Canadian Gun Owners Guide to Election 2019

To Save Your Guns,

Vote Conservative...

Except in the 100 Ridings

Where You Shouldn't

By

Christopher di Armani and Nicolas Johnson

Get Updates and Alerts

Don't miss out on important election news in 2019.

Sign up to receive our updates and alerts
for gun owners directly to your inbox:

VoteGuns.ca

Published By:

Botanie Valley Productions Inc.
PO Box 507
Lytton, BC V0K 1Z0
http://BotanieValleyProductions.com

How to Use This Book

The single most important sentence of this book for you is the voting recommendation for your riding. The rest of the book explains how the authors reached each recommendation and why it matters.

If You Have 2 Minutes

- Go to Chapter 16, Voting Recommendations, find your electoral district and see how to vote to save your guns.
- If you need convincing, read the Quick Responses to FAQs.

If You Have 20 Minutes

- Read the one-page snapshot on Liberal gun bans and our mission strategy on how to save our guns in Election 2019.
- Go to Chapter 16, Voting Recommendations, find your electoral district and see how to vote to save your guns.
- Flip through the Quick Responses to FAQs.

If You Want It All

- Read the book.

Sign up for e-mail updates and alerts: VoteGuns.ca

Election 2019 Mission

The next government of Canada will be Conservative or Liberal.

- If Liberals win, the government will order massive gun bans and new restrictions against PAL/RPAL holders.
- If the Conservatives win, the government won't.

This is the outcome whether you are left or right, libertarian or authoritarian, capitalist or communist, centrist or extremist, regardless of your affinity for or animosity against any specific political party.

Our Mission: Save Our Guns by Defeating Liberals

This book shows you how to vote in your riding to save your guns.

Think team sports. We play offence where we can win and defence where we can't.

Offence: Vote Conservative in the 238 ridings where research and polling data show Conservatives can win.

Defence: In the 100 ridings identified as unwinnable for Conservatives, block the Liberals by voting NDP or Bloc Québécois.

Sign up for e-mail updates and alerts: VoteGuns.ca

Liberal Gun Ban Plan

The Liberal Party of Canada plans new restrictions and prohibitions against gun owners if they win Election 2019, including the biggest round of gun bans and confiscations in Canadian history. Bill Blair, the minister in charge, outlined the measures in mid-June 2019. Here are the highlights. See Chapter 10, Liberal Reality, for all the details.

1. Immediate Surrender: Seize and Destroy

- Order PAL holders to immediately surrender about 200,000 of their legally-purchased rifles and shotguns for destruction. No more slow-motion confiscation, commonly called "grandfathering" — where police wait to seize guns from families after the registered owner dies.
- Offer to pay for surrendered guns.
- Target owners of so-called "Non-Restricted" and "Restricted" models, and possibly "Prohibited" firearms.

2. Ban Gun Owners and Gun Stores From Cities

- Invent new laws for provinces and municipalities to ban firearm owners and gun stores.
- Make it easy to ban handgun owners.

3. Ban or Further Restrict Private Gun Ownership

- Invent new storage laws preventing you from storing your firearms at home.

vi • A MANUAL FOR POLITICAL ACTION

The Liberal Party is campaigning to execute the biggest single gun ban in Canadian history.

The mission of this book is to stop them.

Gun Owners Pledge

"To save our guns and our community, I pledge to vote Conservative in ridings where Conservatives can win, or to vote for the strongest non-Liberal party in ridings where they can't."

Alternate

"God, grant me Serenity to vote Conservative in ridings they can win, Courage to vote NDP or Bloc Québécois where they can't, and Willingness to read this book so I know the difference."

"We look forward to the next time that Parliament is sitting – hopefully under a Liberal government – where we will be able to introduce further measures to strengthen measures against guns."

—Prime Minister Justin Trudeau,
Toronto, August 13, 2019
Source: The Globe and Mail

Table of Contents

"Gun control presents an untapped opportunity for Justin Trudeau and his team to grow and solidify the voting base that gave them a majority in 2015."

—David Rodier and Elliott Gauthier
Hill+Knowlton Strategies
Policy Options, March 9, 2018[1]

Why We Wrote This Book

Our Culture, Our Community, Our Country

We wrote this book because we care about our community: the millions of Canadian men, women and youth who own or use firearms safely and responsibly as good citizens.

Election 2019 will determine whether we have a short or a long future.

Whether you use guns for protection, hunting, plinking, recreation, competing, collecting or any other legitimate purpose, we feel it's important to protect a culture and heritage older than Canada itself.

Our Concern

Over the past few decades, our country has seen the rise of politicians eager to attack the liberty, dignity and rights of our community through deceit, distortion and demonization.

They corrupt our legal system by criminalizing people who are neither immoral nor harmful. (You can go to jail over paperwork, for taking a detour on the way to the target range, for having a standard-sized ammunition magazine, and so much more.)

They demonize good citizens and confiscate our property.

They stop "good guys," because they can. They do nothing to stop "bad guys," because they can't. They work to ban gun ownership by the most-vetted and safest people in the country, but they don't do a thing to ban dangerous, violent criminals — the very people they claim their misguided policies will stop.

These politicians are a threat to the health of our democracy, the safety of our communities and the future of our country.

But ... We don't blame the politicians.

We blame the voters who elect them.

Our Hope

We wrote this book so we could all vote smarter. If we don't, our proven culture of safety, responsibility and good citizenship (along with our guns) will suffer another massive blow in Election 2019, shoving us one step closer to extinction.

If we do vote smarter, Election 2019 could be a turning point.

This book is our attempt to make it one.

Wishing you, your children and your grandchildren many more decades of happy shooting experiences.

Yours in Liberty,

Christopher di Armani   Nicolas Johnson
Lytton, British Columbia   Toronto, Ontario

August 30, 2019

About the Authors

Together, we wrote The Bill C-71 Book and helped make Bill C-71 one of the most-opposed legislative efforts of the outgoing Liberal government.

Christopher di Armani worked in the movie industry for 18 years where, among other duties, he taught actors how to handle firearms properly. He is also a former CFSC/CRFSC firearm safety instructor, is Black Badge certified in IPSC and is an IDPA safety officer instructor.

He published Canadian Rights and Freedoms Bulletin, a free weekly newsletter reporting on our ongoing battle for liberty, from 2010 to 2015.

He also created the "Katey's Firearms Facts" series on YouTube, which was viewed over 1 million times. Along with his three documentary films, these efforts helped raise over $230,000 for a constitutional challenge of the Firearms Act.

He and his wife live in the mountains about three hours from Vancouver.

Nicolas Johnson is the editor of TheGunBlog.ca, Canada's leading media for gun rights.

Tens of thousands of people count on TheGunBlog.ca's independent journalism each week for exclusive news, analysis and insight.

In 2014, Nicolas ran for election to Ontario's legislature. He worked previously as a financial reporter and editor for Bloomberg News in Europe and Asia, followed by a stint at The Globe and Mail in Toronto. He lives in Toronto.

Any gun owner who doesn't vote
by October 21st
should surrender their guns
on October 22nd.

Introduction

Canada's next prime minister will be one of two men: Andrew Scheer or Justin Trudeau. If it isn't Scheer, we can kiss our guns goodbye.

Trudeau's Liberal Party is campaigning on plans for the biggest round of gun bans and confiscations in Canadian history if they win Election 2019.

The Conservative Party, led by Scheer, is the only party with a legitimate chance of forming government and stopping them.

The Liberals, in June 2019, said they want federally licensed firearm owners (PAL and RPAL holders) to turn in about 200,000 of our rifles and/or shotguns for destruction (no "grandfathering"), they want to pass laws to ban handgun owners from big cities and they want to make it harder for us to keep our guns at home.

Anyone owning so-called "Non-restricted," "Restricted" or "Prohibited" rifles, shotguns or handguns is at risk if the Liberals are re-elected. As recently as August 13, 2019, the prime minister said he will campaign on "strengthening gun control" and forming a government "to strengthen measures against guns."

As the authors write these words at the end of August, opinion polls give Trudeau and the Liberals a solid chance of winning in October.

Self-serving politicians have weaponized gun ownership to win votes, and Election 2019 will determine if Canadian gun culture has a long or a short future.

The ideas in this book are designed to stop Liberals from implementing their plans against the honest men and women in our community by preventing them from forming government.

If we accomplish this, we save our guns.

Any new confiscations or restrictions will immediately and directly affect Canada's 2.2 million men and women with a firearm Possession and Acquisition Licence (PAL), such as hunters, farmers, ranchers, sport shooters, plinkers and firearm collectors.

They will force many gun stores, shooting clubs and target ranges to close. They will eliminate shooting disciplines, destroy jobs and kill careers. They will force families to flee the country, surrender their guns, or face jail.

Conservatives can't win in 100 electoral districts.

Those 100 ridings will elect a gun-banning MP.

Will you vote to make sure it's not a Liberal one?

1. Our Mission

In Election 2019 it doesn't matter where we stand politically: left or right, libertarian or authoritarian, capitalist or communist, moderate or extremist. We need to forget about party affiliation and vote tactically. We will either save our guns by working together or we will lose our guns separately.

That's why the authors deliberately set aside ethics scandals, immigration crises, climate emergencies, trips to India, homeless military veterans, runaway debt, broken promises, dairy cartels, or any other topic making headlines each day.

Our only concern in Election 2019 is preventing a Liberal government committed to ending our peaceful firearms community by electing a Conservative government that won't.

This book proposes we play the electoral game intelligently to save our guns. We have an incredible opportunity, but only if we vote smart.

The solution is both complex and simple at the same time. It's complex, because gun owners are an independent lot with strong opinions. It's simple, because if we act together, we can win.

Mission Objective

Our mission objective is to save our guns.

Mission Plan

How do we accomplish this objective? By removing a government that wants to take our guns and electing a government that won't.

Mission Mindset

Let's reframe how we think about elections. Let's view Election 2019 through the lens of team sports, where every gun owner is playing offence or defence in 338 individual games, depending on the political reality of their electoral district.

We take care of the small things by stopping Liberals in the electoral district where we cast our vote. When we do this, the big thing, electing a government favourable to gun owners and gun ownership, takes care of itself.

Situation Report

In colourful terms: Team Blue has the best chance to form government and save our guns. Team Red has the best chance to form government and take away our guns. All other teams, regardless of the colour of their jerseys, cannot form government, making their love or hate for firearm users irrelevant.

Strategy

Help Team Blue players win as many individual games (electoral districts) as they can so they win the National Championship (and form government). In games where Team Blue can't win, work with the team with the best chance of beating Team Red so they lose the National Championship (don't form government).

Methodology

We analyzed Elections Canada data for the results of every riding in every election from 2004 through the 2019 by-elections.

Then we examined the latest opinion polls and projections and factored in any special circumstances (e.g. individual candidates and/or issues) to determine a voting recommendation for each game (electoral district) in the country.

Recommended Action

Based on the latest information available, this team strategy means:

- In 238 games (electoral districts) vote Team Blue
- In 81 games (electoral districts) vote Team Orange
- In 18 games (electoral districts) vote Team Bloc Québécois
- In 1 game (electoral district) vote Independent

Leverage Point

All votes are not equal. Every vote in the 100 games (electoral districts) where we play defence has the potential to change the score (result) of that game and thereby affect the outcome of the National Championship.

Sphere of Influence

Your vote counts.

So do the votes of everyone in your personal sphere of influence: your family, friends, neighbours and co-workers.

Key Risks

- Some gun owners will vote Team Red.
- Some gun owners will vote for fringe parties that will boost Team Red's chances of winning.
- Some gun owners will refuse to follow these recommendations.
- Some gun owners won't vote at all.

Worst Outcome

- Team Red Wins, and we lose.

Best Outcome

- Team Blue Wins, we survive today and prepare for the next battle in four years (or less, in the case of a minority government).

Likely Outcome

The latest opinion polls and seat projections suggest either outcome is possible.

2. Disclosures and Disclaimers

This book analyzes Election 2019 from a single point of view: How to save our community, our guns and our rights. This book is non-partisan. It recommends voting for several major parties.

The authors are both members of the Conservative Party.

The research and conclusions show we both happen to live in ridings where Conservatives might win, so we are both volunteering or getting paid to work on our local campaigns.

We suspect every party's leadership and fans will dislike our message to vote for parties other than their favourite.

That's okay.

We wrote this book independently, on our own initiative and using our resources. Nobody paid us to write it. Nobody told us what to say or how to say it.

We know a lot of gun owners won't like our conclusions.

That's okay, too.

We didn't write this book to be liked.

We wrote this book to save our community, our culture and our guns.

You have thousands of dollars invested in your firearms.

You can't afford to get this election wrong.

3. QRF: Quick Response FAQ

This section lists short responses to common questions and common objections under five headings:

- General
- People's Party of Canada
- Guns and Politics
- The Conservative Party
- Tactical Voting

The rest of the book provides the research, analysis and reasoning behind these brief responses.

General

Is this book relevant to me if I don't own guns? How about if I only own "Non-Restricted" rifles and shotguns?

This book is relevant if you value what firearm ownership represents, whether you own guns or not. It will help you even if you don't care about gun ownership at all, and just want to prevent a Liberal government or elect a Conservative one in Election 2019.

The Liberal Party's plans for the biggest round of gun confiscations in Canadian history include the seizure and destruction of at least 85,000 "Non-Restricted" rifles and shotguns.

If you own guns of any kind, this book is relevant to you.

I usually vote [Insert Party Name Here].

The premise of this book is we must set aside our feelings, party loyalty, party leaders and analyze this election tactically.

We face one of two possible outcomes in Election 2019: a supportive Conservative government or a hostile Liberal one.

Our mission is to save our community, our culture and our guns.

How do we get there? By playing offence and defence.

Offence: In the 238 ridings where the party that won't take our guns (Conservatives) can win, we play offence and vote for them.

Defence: In the 100 ridings where the Conservatives can't win, we play defence. We vote for the party with the best chance of defeating the one that wants to take our guns (Liberals). In those 100 ridings, this means voting NDP, Bloc Québécois, Green or Independent.

See Chapter 16, Voting Recommendations, for how to vote for your guns in your riding.

How should I vote in Election 2019?

Our biggest threat in 2019 is the Liberal Party, since they're campaigning to bring in new measures against us, including the largest round of gun confiscations in Canadian history. The Conservatives won't.

Our mission is to save our community, our culture and our guns, which means voting for the strongest non-Liberal party in every riding. We're playing offence in 70% of ridings and voting Conservative. In the other 30%, we're playing defence by voting for someone else (NDP or Bloc Québécois).

How to vote depends upon your electoral district, so go to Chapter 16, Voting Recommendations, and find your riding. The rest of this book explains the analysis and reasoning behind each one of those electoral recommendations.

Isn't the best way to save our guns simply for everyone to vote Conservative?

We wish there was a single, simple voting solution for all gun owners and users. There isn't.

A simple message like "Everyone Vote Conservative" is a bad strategy because it will hand many ridings (where Conservatives can't win) to the Liberals.

Our goal is to save our community, our culture and our guns by avoiding measures the Liberals have promised against us. It means we need a strong Conservative government and we need to prevent a Liberal one.

Here's how we get there. In the 238 ridings where the Conservatives have a chance of winning, vote Conservative.

In the 100 ridings where the Conservatives are weak and can't win, voting for them risks electing Liberals because the real battle in those 100 ridings is Liberal vs. NDP, Bloc Québécois or Green. Supporting these parties in these 100 ridings is our best chance to defeat Liberals because we're blocking them from getting elected.

See Chapter 16, Voting Recommendations, for how to vote for your guns in your riding.

People's Party of Canada (PPC)

Maxime Bernier and the People's Party of Canada (PPC) have a good firearm policy and offer a better alternative.

I want to send a message against the Liberal-Conservative establishment.

Our electoral system is far from perfect, but the next government will be either Conservative or Liberal. The Conservatives support us in 2019. The Liberals are working against us.

Every poll shows voting PPC hurts our allies, the Conservatives, and helps our adversaries, the Liberals.

The sole mission of this book is to protect civilian firearm owners from a politically hostile government. We provide specific recommendations for every voter in every electoral district to achieve victory, backed up by research and rationale for each recommendation.

If you want to surrender your guns and your liberty, ignore this book's recommendations.

If you want to keep your guns and your rights, don't vote PPC.

What about the Libertarian Party? They have a great platform.

One of the ironies we discovered is Libertarian voters elect Liberals.

The research and analysis shown in this book did not find a single electoral district where voting Libertarian defeated the party that wants to take away our guns, nor did we find a single riding where voting Libertarian helped the party that won't take away our guns.

We discovered two ridings in Election 2015 where voting Libertarian helped defeat Conservatives and elect Liberals and NDP instead. See Chapter 7, Key Ridings Where Gun Owners Can Determine the Winner, for details.

Voting PPC, Libertarian or for other small parties in Election 2019 is an indirect vote for Liberal restrictions, gun bans and confiscations.

Guns and Politics

PAL holders are in every political party. There's nothing "conservative" about hunting, shooting or gun ownership.

A lot of gun owners assume because you own guns you're going to vote for the Conservative Party. That assumption is wrong.

Owning guns is not a conservative thing, it's a Canadian thing. Communists, capitalists, leftists, rightists and centrists all enjoy hunting and sport shooting.

Gun owners and users come from every income level and job description, every social class and educational background, every world-view and political party.

That's the reason for this book's pragmatic approach.

The next government will be either Conservative or Liberal. If it's Liberal, we lose our guns. If it's Conservative, we keep our guns for a few more years.

The mission for every person in every riding is to vote in a way that results in a Conservative government and prevents a Liberal one. This book shows you how to vote offensively or defensively, as required.

Voting NDP, Green or Bloc Québécois is as bad or worse for gun owners than voting Liberal.

PAL holders need to play either offence or defence in Election 2019, depending on your riding. Two different tactics to achieve a single mission: preventing a Liberal government and electing a Conservative one.

In the 238 ridings where Conservatives can win, we play offence and vote Conservative. In the 100 ridings where Conservatives can't win, we play defence to block the Liberals and stop them from taking our guns.

How do we play defence? We vote NDP, Green or Bloc in key ridings so they win instead of the Liberals. This book's research and analysis shows how to vote in every riding.

Ignoring these voting recommendations is a choice, but it's a choice our community may regret on October 22nd, 2019, and never recover from.

The Conservative Party

I don't like the Conservative Party, so why would I want a Conservative government?

The next government will be either Conservative or Liberal.

We'd better make sure it's Conservative, because the Liberals will turn us into former gun owners.

If you value your community, your culture and your guns, and the Conservatives can win your riding, any other vote is a vote against your guns and for Liberal gun bans.

This book's analysis and recommendations show voters how to win.

See Chapter 16, Voting Recommendations, for details on your riding.

The Conservative Party hasn't given us enough good reasons to vote for them.

The Liberals want massive gun bans. The Conservatives don't.

This book's voting recommendations focus on saving our community, our culture and our guns. Winning Election 2019 is just the first step in preserving our community and winning back our rights.

Bigger picture, the Conservative Party can't do anything for anyone if they don't form a strong government.

After the election, it's our job to work with our elected Conservative members of parliament and ministers and hold them accountable so they fulfill their election promises.

See Chapter 15, "We Won, Now What?" for details on how we can and must hold them accountable.

Conservatives had 10 years to fix our broken gun laws and they let us down. Why should I support them now?

This book is for those who want to keep their community, their culture and their guns.

It's not about yesterday, it's about tomorrow.

Firearm owners and enthusiasts have two choices in Election 2019: We can vote in a way that permits Liberals to continue hurting us, or vote in a way that strengthens the Conservatives so we can keep our guns.

Chapter 9, Conservative Party Myths, explores misconceptions about gun owners and the Conservative Party, and reveals some truths about how the party has both hurt and helped the shooting community.

All of that is history. None of it matters when we vote in October.

What matters is preventing a Liberal government that wants to end our community by electing a Conservative government that doesn't.

Tactical Voting

Tactical or Strategic voting doesn't work, does it?

During the 2015 election campaign, "Anyone But Harper" was the battle cry of left-wing voters wanting to end left-wing vote-splitting and get rid of the Conservative government.

Ali Kashani researched and publicized 16 ridings where strategic voting could prevent Conservatives from winning.

"If the Liberal party and NDP cooperate, they can claim these ridings back from the Conservatives, and each can win an additional 8 seats."[2]

In Election 2019, at least 100 ridings will elect a party that wants to ban guns. Our mission is to make sure it's not a Liberal who could form government.

We save our community, our culture and our guns by working with anyone who can defeat the Liberals in those ridings.

"Anyone But Liberal" is our battle cry in Election 2019.

Can the shooting community make a difference in every riding? Maybe not, but we can make a difference in enough ridings to prevent Liberals from winning them.

See Chapter 16, Voting Recommendations, for how to vote in your electoral district.

What's the biggest threat to gun owners?

The biggest threat to gun owners in Election 2019 is ... gun owners. We're disorganized. We're stuck in our own silos. We keep to ourselves. Some of us vote against our own interests. Some PAL holders want gun bans. Some of them will vote Liberal.

What's the biggest hope for gun owners?

The best hope for our community and our culture to survive beyond Election 2019 is to vote like gun ownership matters.

One way is to follow the recommendations in this book.

After the Election

What's the plan after the election?

This book is a guide for how to save our community, our culture and our guns in Election 2019.

Job Number 1 is urgent and immediate.

Defeat the Liberal Party in every riding possible by playing defence in the 100 ridings where it's necessary, and playing offence everywhere else to elect a Conservative majority government.

The book also highlights a few important things all gun owners should consider doing the day after the election, regardless of who wins.

See Chapter 15, We Won, Now What? for more details.

4. Liberals Plan Massive Gun Bans

The Liberals plan the biggest single gun bans in Canadian history if re-elected.

Bill Blair, Trudeau's minister of gun bans and firearm confiscation, officially began exploring massive gun bans against federally licensed firearm owners in August 2018. In June 2019, after 10 months of research and planning, he outlined the Liberal Party's intentions to media, starting with an exclusive interview with The Globe and Mail on June 14, 2019.[3]

Liberal Gun Ban Plan

1. Immediate Surrender — Seize and Destroy Firearms

- Order PAL holders to immediately surrender about 200,000 rifles and shotguns for destruction with no delayed confiscation our enemies call "grandfathering."
- Government may offer to pay for what is turned in.
- Target owners of so-called "Non-Restricted" and "Restricted" models and possibly "Prohibited" as well.

2. Ban Gun Owners and Stores From Cities

- Invent new laws for provinces and municipalities to ban firearm owners and gun stores.
- Make it easy to ban handgun owners.

3. Ban or Further Restrict Private Gun Ownership

- Invent new storage laws to prevent you from storing your guns safely in your own home.

What We Don't Know

Minister Blair spoke to The Globe, the Toronto Star and other media to outline the Liberal Party's plans, but there's a lot he didn't specify.

Targets: A lot of PAL holders assume the Trudeau confiscations will focus on owners of semi-automatic AR-15 target rifles legally classified as "Restricted." That assumption may be right, it may not. Blair didn't specify any model, type or class of firearm.

Triggers: Any government can make owning any gun illegal anytime by a cabinet directive known as an Order in Council (OIC). Will the Liberals, if re-elected, order gun bans overnight by OIC, or will they require new laws approved by parliament? Or both?

Tactics: How will the Liberals enforce their bans against honest families, especially considering police across the country oppose the plans?

Timing: When will the Liberals begin the seizures — the day they take office, or later?

Costs: How much will the Liberals offer for each gun? How will they compensate people for violating our dignity, the years invested in our sport, the accessories they'll render worthless without the gun, or the historical or sentimental value of guns? How will they compensate the businesses they destroy and the people whose jobs they kill?

More Details: The prime minister told media in Toronto on August 13, 2019, he will provide an update on his attack plans against gun owners later in the campaign.[4]

What We Know

What we do know is the Liberals will go after people who own at least 87,000 "Non-restricted" rifles and shotguns. It could be a lot more.

The Math

Blair said the Liberals will seize and destroy about 200,000 firearms that aren't handguns, so he's targeting people who own rifles and/or shotguns.

Canada had about 113,000 "Restricted" and "Prohibited" long guns in private hands at the end of April 2019, according to RCMP data published by TheGunBlog.ca.

200,000 - 113,000 = 87,000

Which "Non-Restricted" firearms?

We don't know, but people are concerned it will be semi-automatic rifles such as the SKS, IWI Tavor and X95, Ruger Mini-14, various KelTec models, and so forth. Possibly shotguns with MIL-STD 1913 rails or magazine-fed shotguns. Maybe some semi-auto shotguns.

The Sky's the Limit

The mass confiscation currently underway in New Zealand shows the Liberal bans could be much broader than what's outlined above.

The New Zealand seizure of "Military-Style Semi-Automatic" Firearms includes everything from centrefire, mag-fed, semi-auto AR-15 target rifles to pump-action shotguns holding more than five rounds, to some bolt-action rifles, chambered for either centrefire or rimfire .22LR.

Minister Blair gave only a rough outline of his boss's intentions. The final plans, should the Liberals win Election 2019, could be much worse.

"We look forward to the next time that Parliament is sitting – hopefully under a Liberal government – where we will be able to introduce further measures to strengthen measures against guns," Trudeau told reporters in Toronto on August 13, 2019.

180 Days to Surrender

You check the mail and notice a letter from the RCMP Canadian Firearms Program. That's odd. You haven't bought or sold any guns recently, and your licence doesn't expire for a while. Your heart pounds as your fingers work the envelope.

The letter is hard to understand. You read it three times. Then you get it. The Liberal government is accusing you of threatening public safety and is ordering you to get rid of your favourite guns within 180 days. Six months.

You've done your best to be a model citizen. You don't understand why they consider you a menace.

You are allowed to take your firearms out of the country before the deadline and leave them abroad (if the other country allows you), you may sell them abroad, or you must surrender them to police for immediate destruction.

If you are caught in Canada with your guns after the deadline, the police will charge you with serious crimes, confiscate your firearms anyway, and throw you in jail.

Why would the Liberals threaten to turn hundreds of thousands of men and women into criminals?

Opinion polls show Liberal voters like gun bans, and the Liberal Party like votes.

5. Political Reality

The Day After: Post-Election Scenarios

Election 2019 has four probable outcomes. Only one of them keeps us safe from Liberal plans to eliminate our community, our culture and our guns from Canada.

1. Liberals win a majority
2. Liberals win a minority
3. Conservatives win a minority
4. Conservatives win a majority

Here's the analysis of what happens in each scenario, from worst to best.

1. Liberals Win a Majority: Worst Outcome

This is the worst-case scenario for civilian gun owners.

If the Liberals form a majority government, they will implement their plans for the broadest crackdown on honest hunters, sport shooters and other firearm users in a generation, as well as the biggest round of gun bans and gun confiscations in Canadian history.

2. Liberals Win a Minority: Bad Outcome

If the Liberals don't win enough seats to form a majority government, they will need the support of another party to remain in power. In this scenario, all options against firearm owners and users are on the table.

Since four of the five main political parties want gun bans of one form or another, a coalition would be a minor inconvenience to stealing our property or forcing us to leave the cities where we live today.

Whether they partner with NDP, Greens or Bloc Québécois, the Liberals could move forward on gun bans as easily as if they had a majority.

A minority Liberal government would probably also remain in power until the next scheduled federal election in 2023.

3. Conservatives Win a Minority: Fragile Outcome

A Conservative minority government opens up another terrifying yet very real possibility. An opposition party, say the Liberals, introduces legislation to ban and confiscate guns. They could gang up against the Conservatives using the NDP, Greens and Bloc Québécois to push this legislation through.

Imagine this nightmare scenario.

Massive gun bans and mass confiscations imposed under a Conservative prime minister. Is this realistic? In our current political climate, yes.

If the Conservative Party forms a minority government, our guns may be safe as long as that government stands. The time frame could be as short as a few months or as long as four years, but whatever length of time it is, we're fighting this battle again in the very near future.

4. Conservatives Win a Majority: Best Outcome

The only way we are safe from government measures against us (until the next election) is if we elect a Conservative majority in 2019.

That's not a message many gun owners want to hear, especially if they feel closer to the NDP, Green Party, Bloc Québécois, People's Party of Canada or any other party.

Like it or not, this is the political reality we face in Election 2019.

6. Forget Your Party and Vote for Your Guns

This is not a "Vote for Party X" or "Don't Vote for Party Y" book.

This is a "Vote for My Guns" book.

Our goal in Election 2019 is simple.

We save our community by electing a government that doesn't want to destroy it, and preventing a government that does.

From the point of view of this book, this is what matters.

To help our minds grasp the essentials of our mission and how to achieve it, let's put aside all the stuff we normally talk about when we discuss elections: personalities, policies, platforms, promises, track records, and all the rest.

The Election Game

Let's look at this election as a competition, a series of small games that determine who wins the National Championship and forms government.

Many Games, One National Championship

Think of a sport where teams compete for a National Championship. Many teams compete against each other in many games or matches. Each team battles all the others for victory.

The team who wins the most games wins the National Championship. They are the heroes who take home the big trophy or, in the case of Liberals, take away our rights, our culture and our guns.

Team Players: Offence and Defence

Each member of our team has a primary role, offence or defence. Offence means you are focused on winning because your job is to score points for your team. Defence means you are focused on not losing, and your job is to stop the other team from scoring points against you.

Offence and defence have separate objectives, tactics and techniques, but everyone on the team is working toward a larger common goal: winning their individual game so we win the National Championship.

Defence wins championships and, by playing defence in 100 electoral districts in Election 2019, we will save our community, our culture and our guns.

Critical Mistake

The best way to lose games (ridings) is to play offence when we should be on defence, or to play defence when we should be on offence. This could cost us the match (riding) as well as the National Championship (government).

If Team Red wins the National Championship and forms government, Team Gun Owner is toast.

One National Champion After 338 Individual Games

The National Championship we're talking about is Election 2019. It is made up of 338 games across the country, one in every electoral district. Every team (party) competes in every district. The team who wins the most matches (districts) wins the championship (forms government).

Unequal Teams

All teams playing for the championship (government) aren't equal. We know the championship will be won by Team Blue or Team Red because they are the strongest. We also know the championship won't be won by Team Orange, Team Green or any other secondary team. Many teams are so small most of us have never heard of them.

We also know each of the major teams will win some games (electoral districts) and lose some games in the 338 total matches.

For example, in the 2015 championship:

- Team Red won 184 matches
- Team Blue took 99
- Team Orange took 44
- Team BQ (Bloc Québécois) took 10
- Team Green took 1

Team Red won the most matches (ridings), so they won the National Championship and formed government.

Team Gun Owner

If you're reading this book, you're on Team Gun Owner. Team Gun Owner is a stealth team. We don't exist officially, but our players are everywhere and we can play (vote) in a way that determines which team wins. Some of us need to play offence, some of us are on defence.

Offence: Focused on Winning

In Election 2019, Team Gun Owner is playing offence in 238 matches (electoral districts). In those matches, Team Gun Owner's objective is to help Team Blue win because Team Blue doesn't want to take away our guns. We vote for Team Blue, volunteer for Team Blue, give money to Team Blue, support Team Blue. (Team Blue = Conservative Party)

Defence: Focused on Not Losing

Team Gun Owner is playing defence in 100 matches (electoral districts). In those matches/ridings, our objective is to block Team Red (Liberal Party), because Team Red is our strongest and fiercest adversary.

If they win the championship, Team Gun Owner loses. So in each match (riding) we play defence by finding the strongest team (riding) who can help us block Team Red. Depending on the match (riding), we work with Team Orange, Team Green, or Team BQ (Bloc Québécois).

When we're on defence, we ignore Team Blue because in those 100 matches (ridings), they're too weak to be a serious contender.

In matches (ridings) where Team Orange has a chance to beat Team Red, we work/vote for Team Orange.

In matches where Team Green has a chance to beat Team Red, we work/vote for Team Green.

In matches/ridings where Team BQ has a chance of beating Team Red, we work/vote for Team BQ.

How We Play Defence

Here's how we play defence in the 100 electoral districts where the Conservatives are weak and unlikely to win.

If Team Red wins your match, and wins enough matches to win the championship, Team Gun Owner is destroyed by the largest round of gun confiscations in Canadian history, and who knows what else?

If Team Orange wins your match/riding, Team Red is left out in the cold. Team Orange won't win enough games (electoral districts) to win the National Championship (form government), but they can win enough games to prevent Team Red from winning it. That's our goal.

What Doesn't Matter

In this example, notice what doesn't matter. The names of team captains (party leaders) don't matter. The names of their star players (candidates) don't matter. Their win/loss history (track record) or political views (campaign platform) don't matter either.

What Does Matter

Only three things matter in this competition:

Support for Gun Owners

We want a champion who accepts gun owners. That's Team Blue.

We want to avoid a champion who is hostile to us. That's Team Red.

Team Strength Overall

We want to focus our attention on the teams that could win the championship. In Election 2019, it's Team Blue or Team Red.

We want to make sure we don't waste our strength by investing in fringe teams that have no chance of winning the championship, let alone a single match.

Team Strength in Each Match

Offence: We want to focus on helping Team Blue win in the 238 matches where they are strong and have a chance at victory.

Defence: We want to focus on blocking Team Red in the 100 matches where Team Blue can't win. We achieve this by working with another team to help them win and defeat Team Red.

"Never doubt that a small group of thoughtful, committed citizens can change the world; indeed, it's the only thing that ever has."

—Margaret Mead, Anthropologist

7. Key Ridings Where Gun Owners Can Determine the Winner

Election 2019 Is Critical

This chapter looks at three ridings to illustrate the point that by playing offence and defence, we can win the National Championship. We can and remove a Liberal government intent on destroying our community and elect a Conservative government that isn't.

It also shows how we hurt ourselves and our community if we don't follow these voting recommendations:

1. Vote Conservative in every riding they can win.

2. In ridings the Conservatives can't win, vote for the strongest non-Liberal party.

3. Voting PPC, Libertarian or other fringe parties boosts the Liberals and risks our guns.

Example: Edmonton Mill Woods (Alberta)

Lesson 1: Every Vote Counts

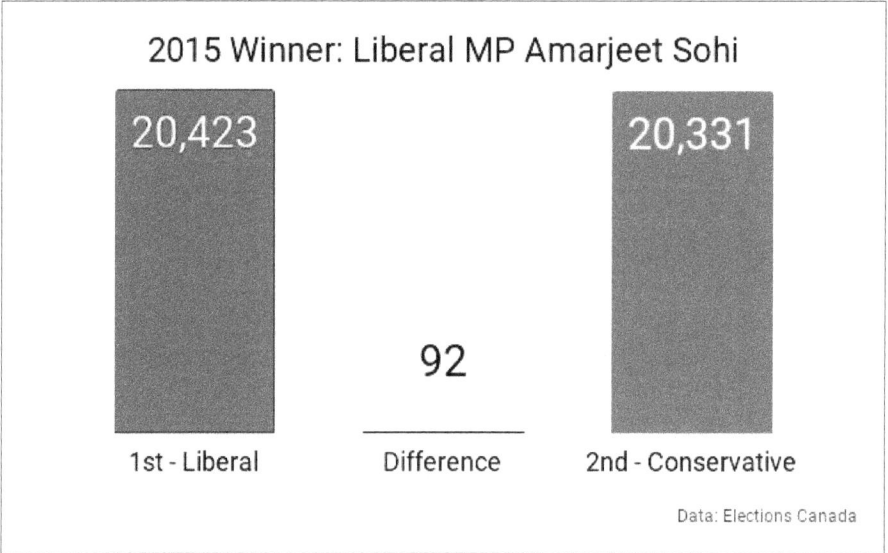

2015 Winner: Liberal MP Amarjeet Sohi

20,423		20,331
	92	
1st - Liberal	Difference	2nd - Conservative

Data: Elections Canada

Imagine you go to bed after the votes are counted on October 21, 2019, and the Liberals won your riding by 92 votes. How would you feel?

That's how a lot of gun users and others must have felt in 2015 in the electoral-district of Edmonton Mill Woods, Alberta. If 93 of them voted smarter (or perhaps voted at all), they would have changed the result. Instead, those 93 men and women (perhaps all PAL holders?) pushed Liberal Amarjeet Sohi to victory.

In Election 2019, failing to vote is voting to fail. Every vote counts.

Lesson 2: Voting for Fringe Parties Elects Liberals

This is an easy problem to fix. The chart below shows more data from the 2015 results. Had right-leaning voters in Edmonton Mill Woods cast ballots for 80% of something they could live, with they would have elected a Conservative MP. Instead they voted for a candidate with zero chance of winning, and ended up with 100% of nothing.

Voting for Fringe Parties Elects Liberals

20,423		20,331		
	92		396	285
1st - Liberal	Difference	2nd - Conservative	6th - Libertarian	7th - Christian Heritage

Data: Elections Canada

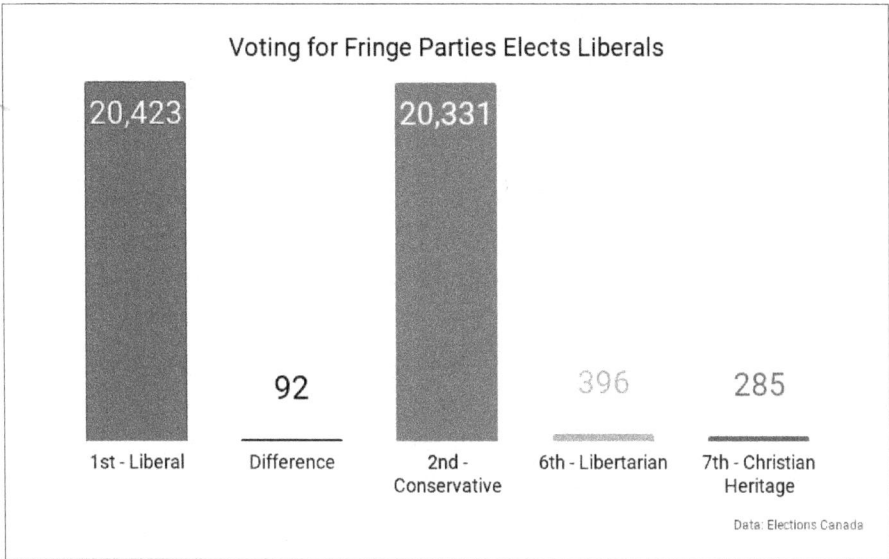

Lesson 3: Where Conservatives Can't Win, We Play Defence

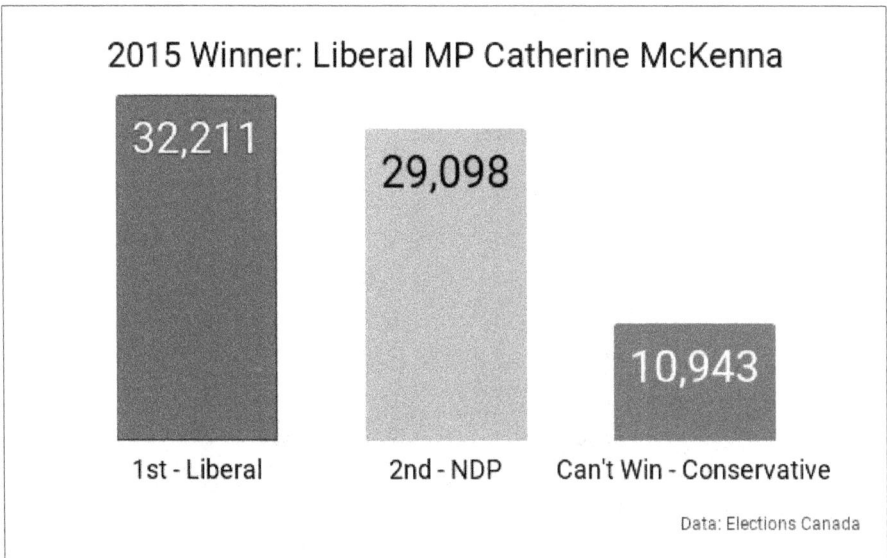

2015 Winner: Liberal MP Catherine McKenna

32,211	29,098	10,943
1st - Liberal	2nd - NDP	Can't Win - Conservative

Data: Elections Canada

Research suggests the Conservatives are unlikely to win in 100 electoral districts. These are almost all ridings where the Conservatives haven't come first or second in at least the past five elections. Sometimes they're in a weak third place, if they make third place at all.

Current opinion polls suggest they'll lose those ridings again this time.

Voting Conservative in these ridings in Election 2019 is a vote to lose our guns. What we should do instead is vote for the strongest non-Liberal party, so we can defeat the Liberals in each of those ridings.

Example: The Liberals won the riding of Ottawa Centre, Ontario, in 2015 with 32,211 votes, almost 11% more than the second-place finisher, the NDP at 29,098. The Conservatives were a distant third with 10,943 and no chance of winning.

Given the Liberals are planning massive gun bans and have a strong chance to form government, the smart thing to do in Election 2019 in such cases is to back the NDP to block the Liberals.

In 2015, failing to vote tactically elected Liberal Catherine McKenna.

Will Election 2019 be different?

Where the Conservatives can't win, play defence and vote NDP, Green, Bloc Québécois or Independent.

See Chapter 16, Voting Recommendations, for which party to vote for in your riding, based on whether you're playing offence or defence.

8. Why Gun Owners Need a Strong NDP

Gun owners would benefit from a strong New Democratic Party in 2019, not because of their firearm policy (which is bad), but because they'd steal ridings from Liberals who want to steal our guns.

Our biggest threat in Election 2019 is a Liberal government.

The Liberal threat is increased by the lackluster state of today's NDP because Conservatives typically win when the NDP achieves 20% of the popular vote, an unlikely scenario in Election 2019.

A stronger NDP would pull votes away from the Liberals, reducing the risk of Liberal gun confiscations. The Greens aren't doing that.

"A lukewarm Conservative leader combined with a weak NDP leader (including what appears to be a complete collapse in seat-rich Québec) should objectively be the perfect electoral scenario for any Liberal prime minister," said Philippe Fournier, the creator of poll aggregator 338Canada.com, on August 15, 2019, in Maclean's magazine.[5]

The NDP favours banning guns from PAL holders, so we don't want them so strong they form government.

We want them just attractive enough to spread left-leaning voters across several parties so they steal seats from Liberals or allow Conservatives to win more seats by splitting the vote.

No party except the NDP is pulling votes from the Liberals.

The Greens are drawing votes from the NDP. They don't threaten a single Liberal riding anywhere in the country.

In the four electoral districts where the Greens are expected to win or be in a coin-flip race, they face NDP incumbents, not Liberals.

This means big danger for us.

We need smaller left-of-centre parties to pull votes away from the Liberal Party, not trade them among each other.

Historical analysis further suggests the weak NDP hurts gun owners.

Eric Grenier, poll analyst for CBC News, looked at past results and found when the NDP did well, so did the Conservatives.

"Two of the three majority governments the Conservatives have secured since 1962 coincided with the NDP's best ever results," Grenier said in November 2018.[6]

9. Conservative Party Myths

The shooting community clings to a few myths about the Conservative Party, and those myths have the potential to damage our relationship with them.

Myth 1:   The Conservative Party Is The Party Of Gun Owners

The first myth is the Conservative Party is the natural or traditional party of gun owners. This is false. While the Conservatives are the natural party for many of us, we typically mistake our support of the party with the Conservative Party's support of us.

Put another way, just because most gun owners vote for the Conservative Party doesn't mean most Conservative Party voters are gun owners.

Every political party has its share of hunters, sport shooters and firearm owners and users.

Myth 2: The Conservative Party Likes Us

In Election 2019, they are our best hope. But they haven't always been our friends. In the 1990s the Conservatives, under Prime Minister Brian Mulroney, banned standard-capacity ammunition magazines for most popular handguns and rifles, and expanded mass confiscation of certain semi-auto rifles, but only after the registered owner dies.

The injustice was led by Justice Minister Kim Campbell. She said on Twitter in May 2019, she was "proud" of the measures she introduced to criminalize honest men and women in our community.[7]

Myth 3: The Conservative Party Knows Us

Most Conservative voters are unfamiliar with the culture of the firearms community. Fewer than 2.2 million men and women have a firearm Possession and Acquisition Licence, out of an estimated 29 million eligible voters.

That means 92% of eligible voters don't know about guns, don't care much about guns or recognize the value and benefits of owning guns. Assume this percentage holds in every political party, including the Conservatives.

Christopher (co-author of this book) lives in the mostly rural British Columbia riding of Mission–Matsqui–Fraser Canyon. He experienced this unfamiliarity with hunting and shooting two years ago after he asked his Conservative Electoral District Association (EDA) how he could help them.

A few board members had a passing familiarity with gun ownership and gun politics, but didn't own guns at the time and also didn't appreciate the value and benefits of firearm ownership.

The board invited him to give a 5-minute presentation on guns and gun politics. Then they asked him questions for half an hour. They eventually invited him to join the board and to serve on the campaign team. He accepted both positions.

Myth 4: The Conservative Party Owes Us

No, they really don't. We need to give the Conservative Party a reason to take up our cause before they'll stick out their necks for us. We haven't done that in any significant way.

Politicians can't accomplish anything if they don't form government, which is why we're seeing massive spending announcements. Candidates promise everyone everything if they think it will buy them a vote.

They need votes. The shooting community as a whole has, historically, failed to deliver for the Conservatives. We need to in Election 2019.

Many hunters and target shooters believed Conservative Prime Minister Stephen Harper let them down, that he didn't deliver.

Some prominent gun owners felt so burned they actively worked to defeat the Conservatives in Election 2015. One leader in the gun-rights community ran against the Conservative candidate in his riding. One gun group promoted the slogan of ABC, "Anyone But Conservative" and cheered publicly when the Conservatives lost the election.

The Conservative Party doesn't owe us anything. They have no reason to pay attention to us until we deliver enough votes to help them win.

Once in power, the onus is on us to make sure they deliver on their promises. If we want to gain the ear of our politicians, the very best way to do that is outlined in the chapter We Won, Now What?

On the Other Hand

The Conservatives under Harper achieved two important victories, unique among industrialized countries. They got rid of some of the wasteful bureaucracy around firearm ownership and use.

First, in 2012, they eliminated the useless and error-ridden national police database of rifles and shotguns, what they called the "Long Gun Registry."

Then, in 2014, they introduced Bill C-42 to streamline bureaucratic processes like getting permission to take a firearm to a shooting range, and allowing the government to move specific firearm models up or down the classification scale. Both of these improvements were undone by the Liberals through Bill C-71.

Without erasing past wrongs by former Conservative leaders, we should acknowledge these important wins.

Most importantly to Election 2019, the Conservatives under Andrew Scheer are the only major party standing up for our culture, our heritage and our community. They regularly oppose bans aimed at lawful gun owners. Their pledge to repeal Bill C-71, if elected, was one of their first election promises.

Immediate Confiscation, Not 'Grandfathering'

Thousands of PAL holders bought AR-15 target rifles in May and June 2019 on speculation the Liberals would order bans on new purchases while allowing existing owners to keep their guns until death.

They expected to benefit from a so-called "grandfather clause" for slow-motion confiscations if the Liberals arbitrarily changed the legal label of AR-15s from "Restricted" to "Prohibited."

For many shooters, buying an AR-15 was an expensive protest message, since most AR-15s cost more than $1,500.

These buyers turned out to be wrong.

The Liberals will order them to immediately surrender their guns to police for destruction, to leave the country with their guns or sell them abroad, or face serious criminal charges and jail.

10. Liberal Reality

Hostile Political Force

From the point of view of the hunting and shooting community, which is the only concern of this book, the Liberal Party of Canada is the most hostile political force against our culture, our heritage and our survival.

They have pushed their prohibitionist agenda for decades, and their latest plans (see Chapter 4) show they're just getting started.

They advertise gun bans and firearm confiscations as "public safety" measures but public safety is improved when governments crack down on law-breakers, not the law-abiding.

So why would the Liberals promise a crackdown against millions of honest men and women who hunt and shoot their firearms safely and responsibly, who enjoy plinking with family and friends on weekends, competing in shooting sports, or who value guns as art collections, history or investments?

Politics. To be more specific, votes.

Bans for Votes

Gun bans are a proven vote winner for the Liberals. The party is betting they will be an election winner in 2019. Opinion polls consistently show Liberal voters, especially women, are the most hostile to firearm owners and the most in favour of bans.

Gun Bans + Gender Politics = Votes

"Gun control presents an untapped opportunity for Justin Trudeau and his team to grow and solidify the voting base that gave them a majority in 2015," a government adviser said in March 2018. "Over and above any electoral potential that exists for gun control, it remains an important gender issue."

Source: David Rodier and Elliott Gauthier, Hill+Knowlton Strategies, Policy Options Magazine, March 9, 2019[8]

Exploiting Fear and Ignorance

Critics rightfully say poll respondents don't know guns, don't know gun owners and don't know the laws on gun ownership. They say the poll results are flawed because they ask simplistic questions of non-experts on an incredibly complex portion of criminal law. Polls even show the less respondents know about guns, the more they favour bans. Flawed polls make for bad policy and intentionally biased results.

This may all be correct, but from the point of view of winning elections, it doesn't matter. The Liberals and other political parties are happy to exploit fear and ignorance to win votes.

The bottom line is Liberal voters like gun bans and will vote Liberal to get them. The Liberals might even win Election 2019 because of them.

One-Way Ban Ratchet

It gets worse. In the current political climate no future Conservative prime minister would dare reverse a national ban, even if it targets only good people approved by the federal police.

Opposition parties, hostile media, and activists against gun owners would blame every death-by-bullet on whoever repealed a ban. As the current debate shows, politicians and media are happy to sacrifice honesty to push their agenda.

No prime minister would willingly invite so much negative press. The gun-ban ratchet moves only one way. It only allows for the tightening of restrictions against law-abiding Canadians.

(Side Note: That's what made Conservative Prime Minister Stephen Harper so exceptional in one regard. He scrapped what many people called the "Long-Gun Registry," making Canada one of the only industrial countries to eliminate a wasteful and costly policy related to firearm ownership.)

Other Measures: Bill C-71

The Liberals' sweeping new measures against PAL holders are on top of prohibitions and restrictions in Bill C-71, the new Liberal law against gun owners and firearm retailers.

It bans the sale of specific rifles and confiscates others from grieving families after the registered owners die.

It criminalizes every PAL holder who sells or gives away any firearm, even a "Non-restricted" rifle or shotgun, to any other PAL holder without explicit permission from the federal police (RCMP).

Example: a husband with a PAL gives a gun to a licensed wife or adult child, without specific approval from the RCMP? They both go to jail.

It contains many other measures to criminalize honest firearm owners and users, and only honest firearm owners and users.

History of Contempt

This isn't the first time the Liberals have sought to trample gun owners into the ground.

For decades the party has aggressively pushed for ever-more restrictions and prohibitions.

The Liberals under Prime Minister Jean Chrétien passed the Firearms Act of 1995 and changes to the Criminal Code to criminalize people even if they didn't do anything immoral or harmful. Forget to inform the federal police within a month after you change address, or take a detour on the way to the handgun range, and you could be on your way to jail.

In 2005, Paul Martin, Liberal Party leader at the time, campaigned on eliminating handgun ownership.

The party's 2015 election platform promised to invent new crimes against all firearm owners. Many of those promises turned into Bill C-71, which was officially passed into law in June 2019.

Liberals, NDP, Bloc Québécois and Greens All Want Bans

The Liberal Party isn't the only party seeking to harass responsible firearm users. The NDP, Greens and Bloc Québécois are, too. In the early 1990s, the Conservative Party also passed laws to criminalize honest gun owners.

The current leader, Andrew Scheer, is firmly on the side of gun owners.

What Is a Ban?

A ban is when the government makes you a criminal for having something. Main options in case of bans:

   1. Surrender your things to police.

   2. Don't surrender them, either by leaving your country with your things and living somewhere else as a refugee, or by staying home and keeping your things (at the risk of being charged with a serious crime and going to jail.)

Many people point out the irony of armed police enforcing gun bans. They use their guns to take away your guns.

"Gun bans" aren't gun bans. They're just gun bans for you.

Prohibition and confiscation can be immediate, like what New Zealand is doing following the March 2019 massacre. Or they can be like the slow-motion bans that Canada sometimes does: classify things as "Prohibited" today, confiscate them from your family later, after you die.

The government advertises this as "grandfathering."

Grandfathers are jolly old men. Confiscating your guns after you die isn't "grandfathering." It's confiscating your guns after you die.

11. Bernier Is Bad News for Gun Owners

> "Maxime Bernier and I are very good friends … we don't agree on anything, except that we agree he's going to keep Andrew Scheer from forming government because he's going to split the vote on the right."
>
> —Green Party Leader Elizabeth May
> Mission, BC, March 31, 2019

Maxime Bernier and his fledgling new People's Party of Canada (PPC) are one of the biggest threats to Canadian gun owners in Election 2019.

His danger isn't ideological, it's electoral. Voting PPC will take away ridings from the Conservatives and elect Liberals instead, as voting for right-of-centre fringe parties did in Election 2015.

The bottom line is simple. A vote for Bernier in Election 2019 is a vote against gun owners. It's a vote against yourself, your values, your culture.

How Voting PPC Will Cost Us Our Guns

To test the research and conclusions of this book and make sure the Voting Recommendations are robust, the authors ran a series of "what if" simulations. Based on the PPC's national support level of 3%, drawn primarily from the Conservative Party of Canada (CPC) we wondered what impact PPC would have had on 2015 election results.

Simulations for every one of the 338 ridings in Canada didn't find a single case where voting PPC improved the outlook for PAL holders. The deeper the analysis, the clearer the conclusion: voting PPC in Election 2019 will hurt us.

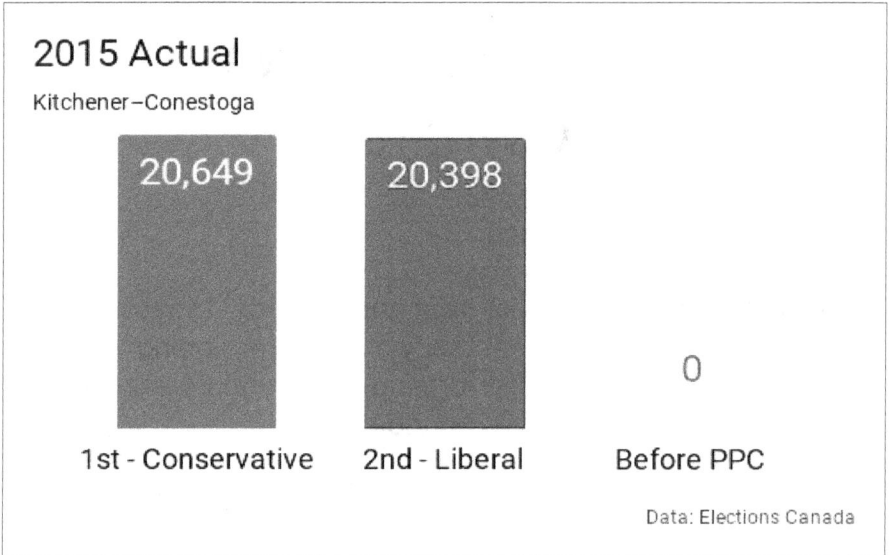

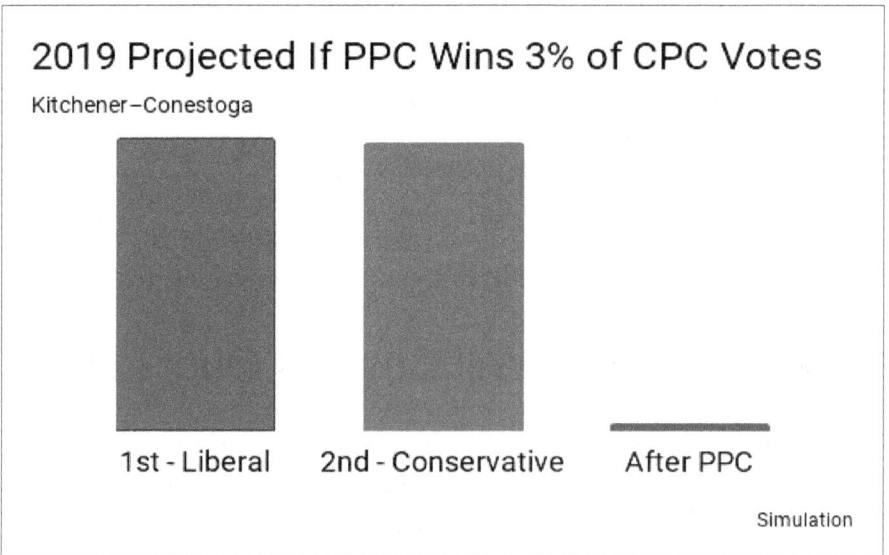

2015 Actual

Kitchener–Conestoga

20,649	20,398	0
1st - Conservative	2nd - Liberal	Before PPC

Data: Elections Canada

2019 Projected If PPC Wins 3% of CPC Votes

Kitchener–Conestoga

1st - Liberal	2nd - Conservative	After PPC

Simulation

Small Party, Big Damage

The good news is the PPC is tiny, so it may not help the Liberals too much since many voters have never heard of Bernier or his movement. The PPC never exceeded 3.1% in three of four by-elections in 2019.

Aggregate projections by 338Canada.com as of August 30, 2019, show the PPC at 2.7% nationally, behind the Conservatives, Liberals, Greens, NDP and Bloc Québécois. They probably won't win a single seat, and election forecasters project Bernier will lose his own district.[9]

3 Percent

The latest polls show the Conservatives and Liberals neck and neck, with each side forming government depending on the poll and the date.

The bad news is almost 3% of voters will vote PPC. That's enough to prevent a Conservative win and elect Liberals instead.

Shaving off 3% of Conservative support is the difference between:

- winning or losing several ridings
- winning or losing the election
- keeping or losing your guns

Voting PPC = Voting for Gun Bans

The risk is real. Based on 2015 election results, a PPC at 3% back then would have delivered three Conservative ridings to the Liberals:

- Barrie–Springwater–Oro-Medonte (Ontario),
- Kitchener–Conestoga (Ontario)
- Montmagny–L'Islet–Kamouraska–Rivière-du-Loup (Québec)

In elections prior to 2015, the Conservatives would have lost six to eight electoral districts. This is how a vote for the PPC is an indirect vote for the Liberals and their plans against the firearms community.

When we say a vote for Maxime Bernier is a vote for the Liberal Party, this is what we mean.

Vote Splitting

Bernier knows his party hurts the Conservatives and made vote-splitting a pillar of his campaign. He is so committed to dividing and destroying the Conservatives, at any cost, he's willing to give the Liberals a second term in government.

In a February 2019 interview for the Toronto Sun, Anthony Furey asked Maxime Bernier how he would feel if he woke up the morning after the 2019 election and learned Trudeau was re-elected as prime minister, partly because of him.

"That can happen," Bernier said.[10]

'I (Used to) Love Mad Max'

Bernier's passion, charisma and views are compelling. It's why one of the authors of this book supported him during the leadership election for the Conservative Party in May 2017.

But this book is focused on the future, not the past. Without a strong Conservative government after Election 2019, our future as Canadian firearm owners looks bleak and short.

Some centre-right voters are turned on at the idea of the PPC as a "real" and "fresh" libertarian-conservative party. They like the party's gun policies and its attacks against "Liberal-Conservatives." They like Bernier's straight talk and his politically incorrect Twitter posts.

Some PPC fans are turned off by the perceived betrayals of firearm owners by the Conservatives, their support of the dairy lobby, or any one of a dozen of other reasons.

Maybe the PPC is at the start of a long and successful reign. We don't know and, more importantly, this book doesn't take an opinion on those topics for Election 2019. It simply analyzes the history of voting results and the more recent forecasts to conclude voting PPC will probably strengthen the Liberals and risk the biggest round of gun confiscations in Canadian history.

Bernier's French Hoax

Some PPC fans believe the polls are wrong and Bernier could become prime minister in Election 2019. Bernier himself promoted this hoax at the beginning of his campaign. He pointed to French President Emmanuel Macron to illustrate how a political outsider can rise to the head of government in less than a year.

Bernier ignored a critical difference in France's electoral system. Each citizen casts a direct ballot for a presidential candidate. That's not how it works in Canada. We vote for a party in our riding. The party who wins the most districts (has the broadest support nationwide) forms the government. The leader of the winning party becomes prime minister. It won't be Bernier in Election 2019.

Conservative Losses When PPC Draws Away 3% Support

Estimated Effect on Past Elections

2015: Conservatives lose 3 ridings, Liberals gain 3.
2011: Conservatives lose 7 ridings, Liberals gain 4, NDP gain 3.
2008: Conservatives lose 6 ridings, Liberals gain 5, NDP gain 1.
2006: Conservatives lose 6 ridings, Liberals gain 5, Bloc gain 1.
2004: Conservatives lose 8 ridings, Liberals gain 4, NDP gain 4.

Bye-Bye Bernier in Beauce

Before doing their research, the authors expected polls to forecast Bernier's victory in his home riding of Beauce, Québec. That's not what's happening. Polling data aggregated by 338Canada.com (August 30, 2019) show a PPC loss and a Conservative victory by 4%,[11] a gap that's grown since November of last year. Should Bernier lose Beauce, which is a real possibility, the People's Party of Canada could disappear just as quickly as it arrived on the political scene.

Police Oppose Trudeau-Tory Gun Bans

The police movement against the Trudeau-Tory gun bans has grown over the past year.

Here are eight of the most powerful police leaders and departments who don't support criminalizing men and women who hunt and shoot safely and responsibly:

- Brenda Lucki, RCMP Commissioner
- Adam Palmer, President of Canadian Association of Chiefs of Police; Vancouver Police Chief
- Mark Saunders, Toronto Police Chief
- Evan Bray, Regina Police Chief
- Danny Smyth, Winnipeg Police Chief
- Chris Lewis, Ontario Provincial Police Commissioner (Rtd)
- Halifax Regional Police
- Mark McCormack, Toronto Police Association President

Source: TheGunBlog.ca

12. Toronto Mayor Tory Threatens All Gun Owners

Tory Attacks Firearm Owners Nationwide

Even though this book focuses on the federal election, threats to good people and good policy exist at all levels of government.

One of the top dangers is John Tory, mayor of Toronto, Canada's largest city. He's one of the most aggressive campaigners against hunters, farmers, ranchers, sport shooters and firearm collectors. The national mass media, most of which are based a few blocks from Toronto City Hall, amplify Tory's hostility across the nation.

In 2014, during his first successful run for mayor, Tory campaigned against the gun bans sought by his opponent, Olivia Chow. He called her idea an "empty gesture."

The second time around, his campaign manager saw a tragedy to exploit, so Tory flipped his position.

In July 2018, a man killed or wounded more than a dozen people on Toronto's Danforth Avenue. The mass media ramped up their campaign to criminalize PAL holders.

Tory surfed the hate wave. He asked sport shooters to leave town. Not once has Tory ever asked drug dealers, gangs, murderers and terrorists to leave the city.

Instead, he asked the federal government to seize every handgun, every semi-automatic rifle and every shotgun from every licensed gun owner across Canada, and to prohibit new sales to civilians.

A month later, the federal Liberals said they might.

On August 5, 2019, Tory renewed his call to criminalize licensed gun owners across Canada, while demanding the federal government confiscate our handguns, semi-automatic rifles (what he calls "assault weapons") and shotguns.[12]

Approximately 100,000 men and women living in Toronto have a firearm licence, one of the highest concentrations of licenced owners anywhere in Canada.

Toronto will elect 25 members of parliament in Election 2019.

Imaginary Letter From 2014 Candidate John Tory to 2018 Mayor John Tory

Dear Mayor Tory,

It's been a while since we talked. You probably don't even remember me. I'm the guy who stood up for law-abiding citizens when Olivia Chow wanted to throw them to the wolves during Toronto's 2014 mayoral election.

"There's no reason why anyone needs a handgun in a big city like ours," she said.

Chow, then running for the job you hold today, wanted to scapegoat Toronto's legal gun owners as part of her election platform.

But me? I refused to allow it.

"Handguns are already strictly regulated by the federal government. What Ms. Chow doesn't seem to understand is that criminals and gang members don't obey the law. Calling for such a ban isn't leadership. It's an empty gesture."

That was my written response.

Do you remember that, John?

Back then, I was the principled voice of reason. I was so proud to stand up for decent Torontonians, not because of the political race, but because it was the right thing to do. But you, Mayor Tory, you've lost your way. When I heard you echo Olivia Chow's statement almost word for ignorant word I was horrified.

"Why does anyone in this city need to have a gun at all?" you asked.

My response to Ms. Chow's insanity then is an equally fitting rebuke of yours today.

Ontario Premier Doug Ford, in response to your call for a handgun ban, said, "We have to refocus all our resources going after the bad guys, not the good guys."

Back in 2014, Mayor Rob Ford accused Olivia Chow of "political grandstanding." Do you see the irony of Rob Ford's brother, our new premier, calling you out for the same grandstanding? Probably not.

Four short years ago you demolished Olivia Chow when you pointed out the obvious, that "criminals and gang members don't obey the law."

Today, you embraced the mantra of her failed mayoral campaign. There is a lesson in that sentence, John, if you're willing to pay attention.

My heart broke when you said, "if it's someone who's involved in a gun club, perhaps they could do that somewhere else." You asked the honest, responsible citizens to leave Toronto, but not drug dealers, gang members, murderers or terrorists.

Honestly, John, I'm ashamed to see what's become of you in four short years. Deeply ashamed. But I'm also hopeful. I hope I can remind you of who you were so you can be that strong voice of reason again.

I pray you find the courage to tackle the hard issues the way we used to, back in the days when we called for the expulsion of evil elements from our society, not our most lawful citizens.

"Criminals and gang members don't obey the law. Calling for such a ban isn't leadership. It's an empty gesture."

You had such courage once, John. It's not too late to find it again.

Yours truly,

The Spirit of 2014 Candidate John Tory

"Law-abiding Canadians should not have to justify to the government why they need a firearm.

You can be assured that I will always be on the side of law-abiding gun owners."

—Andrew Scheer, 2017

13. The Biggest Opportunity for Gun Owners

Will Election 2019 Be a Turning Point?

A key message of this book is the hope Election 2019 will be a turning point for the shooting community and the firearm industry — if we choose to make it one.

It's an opportunity for the millions of men and women who own and use firearms to work together for our common good, to vote smart and show our voice and our vote count.

Our Own Worst Enemy

We haven't always been very good at doing that, and sometimes we've been downright terrible. It's easy to blame the government, mass media, or anyone else for the assault on our freedom, dignity, privacy and guns.

We need to recognize our own responsibility. The biggest threat to gun owners is ... gun owners.

As individuals, we hide in the gun closet.

We keep to ourselves for privacy and security, and to avoid dirty looks from our adversaries. We don't share our shooting interests with family, friends, colleagues or community.

We've allowed ourselves to be divided into PAL holders vs. RPAL holders, into opposing clans and silos who don't look beyond the limits of their own province or region, their own club, their own shooting disciplines.

Many of us don't vote, or we vote for fringe parties that lead to hostile governments. Many firearm users will vote Liberal in Election 2019, and complain about new restrictions and gun bans later.

As businesses, gun stores, target ranges, gun clubs, outfitters, guides, instructors and trainers, too many of us are absent from the public debate.

Many refuse to speak up and refuse to tell members or clients about what's happening politically and legislatively.

Many are run by incompetent and/or rude executives who chase away new shooters.

It's no wonder our community is struggling to survive.

Every day is a chance to change all that, including today.

14. Conclusion

How we vote in Election 2019 will determine the future of civilian firearm owners and users in our country.

If re-elected, the Liberal Party will impose the biggest round of firearm confiscations in Canadian history on the families of hundreds of thousands of honest citizens.

Our job is to stop them.

The voting recommendations in this book are based on election results for every electoral district in every federal election since 2004 plus the latest polls.

Election 2019 offers us the same choice we have every election — support a party or a person we like and avoid a party or a person we don't, or vote tactically to save our community, our culture and our guns.

Yes, even when it means plugging our noses to achieve the mission.

The game plan is simple.

The Liberals want to take our guns, the Conservatives don't. In ridings where the Conservatives can win, we play offence and vote for them. In ridings where they can't win, we play defence and stop Liberals.

Simple.

And beyond the obviously critical results, this election is a wonderful opportunity for our fragmented community to unify and defend our common interests.

This election is not really about guns and our right to own them.

In one way it's not even about our community, our history or our long and storied culture of safety.

Election 2019 will show us and the world what we, as Canadian gun owners and users, want.

Do we prefer politicians who consistently act against their own citizens, or will we elect a government that respects its citizens.

The core of Election 2019 goes so much deeper than the future of our firearm community. It goes to the heart of our democracy.

The world is run by those who show up.

Will you join us?

Yours in Liberty,

Christopher di Armani   Nicolas Johnson
Lytton, British Columbia   Toronto, Ontario

15. We Won, Now What?

Election 2019 is a beginning, not an end. It's the first step on the road to protecting our community from hostile future governments. And there's a good chance a hostile government will resume power in October.

The World Is Run By Those Who Show Up

Even if the Conservatives win this one, we need to do more than just win elections. We need to change the culture. That means sharing the value and benefit of hunting and shooting with more people, being far more active in associations, community groups, media, and businesses.

It means coming out of the gun closet.

The reality of being a firearm owner and user today is when we don't bother to show up, we put our future into the hands of political enemies who want us eliminated.

When we do show up, we can create a future that values, respects, and promotes our community and our culture. Here are a few ideas.

Show Up for Your Candidate

Every candidate needs help. They need volunteers, donations and votes. Campaigns depend on teams to manage people, run databases, make phone calls, hand out flyers, install lawn signs, drive voters to the polls, and so much more. Whatever your personality or skills, contact your candidate, get on their mailing list and help them win. They need you.

Show Up for Your Riding Association

Volunteering for your candidate and/or the electoral district association (EDA) is a good way to boost your credibility and influence.

Who is your candidate and future member of parliament more likely to listen to and trust: a stranger they met once for 20 seconds at a summer BBQ, or someone they've known for years who was critical to their election victory?

Some EDAs are well-run and well-funded, with active members who recruit top-notch candidates. Many EDAs are a mess, on life support. All of them could use you on the board of directors or as a volunteer, depending on your commitment and availability.

Show Up for Your Member of Parliament

Fixing Canada's gun laws is both critical and urgent, and changing the culture will take decades. After the election we need to show up for our Conservative MPs and government ministers in at least two ways:

1. Support their work and attend their events
2. Hold them accountable for fulfilling their election promises.

Show Up By Running for Office

You can show up by running as a candidate yourself.

Show Up Your Way

These are just a few ways to get involved in politics, but politics might not be your thing. Wherever you are, whatever you do, you can play a role by standing up for our community and speaking out in a way that is both authentic and appropriate to your audience and the context of your interaction with them.

More Info

For more information and ideas, download the free PDF booklet:

VoteGuns.ca/ShowUp

16. Voting Recommendations

Recommendations By Province

An overview of the methodology begins on the next page.

How to Use This Guide

Find Your Electoral District / Riding

Ridings change names and/or boundaries in every election. Please check the Elections Canada website's Voter Information Service.

Go to Elections.ca.

In the upper left, click Voters > Voter Information Service

Methodology

Elections Canada Data and How We Crunched It

To decide our voting strategy and recommendation for each riding in Election 2019, we reviewed historical trends, the latest opinion polls and projections, and any other public information that might be relevant.

General Approach

We analyzed each party's result in each riding in the past five general elections, as well as for all by-elections held in between general elections.

We focused on which party won the election in each riding and who placed second. We looked for patterns, giving more weight to more recent elections, so a 2015 or 2019 by-election result carries greater weight than the 2004 result.

Data Source

We obtained raw data for every riding from Elections Canada. We then ran our own calculations and comparisons. In cases of discrepancies between the raw data and published results on the Elections Canada website, we used the raw data.

Complexities and Assumptions

We followed Elections Canada for identifying ridings, including names and numbers. This creates complexities when comparing results from one election to the next, and even more complexities when comparing five elections. Ridings change names and/or boundaries in every election. Some ridings keep the same name while their boundaries keep changing. Ridings are created, merged, split or disappear.

All of these changes make apples-to-apples comparisons difficult from one election to the next, and much more complex over five elections.

How We Determined Voting Recommendations

We recommend voting for the strongest non-Liberal Party in every riding. We recommend voting for the Conservative Party where they placed first or second in the past election, are projected to win in 2019, or where it's a toss up.

In some ridings, the Conservatives haven't come first or second in any election in more than 15 years. Unless polls or news suggest a significant shift, we considered these ridings unwinnable for the Conservatives in Election 2019.

Check the Latest Polls

This book is a guide, and we believe it is the best voting guide of its kind for Election 2019. We recommend you check the latest polls for how to vote in your riding. Where the Conservatives are projected to win or have a good chance, vote Conservative. Where they have a slim or no chance, vote for the strongest non-Liberal party.

We found poll aggregator 338Canada.com to be a useful resource.

Summary

To save our guns, we recommend voting Conservative in 238 ridings, NDP in 81 ridings, Bloc Québécois in 18 ridings and an Independent candidate in 1 riding, as they have the best chance to prevent a Liberal government and elect a Conservative one, and thereby accomplish our mission.

Disclosures and Disclaimers

- Our analysis is current as of August 30, 2019.
- Most ridings had a clear trend, such as consistently electing a single party, or alternating between two parties.
- Some ridings didn't show a clear trend. We suggest checking the news and latest polling results.
- We expect last-minute changes. Go to VoteGuns.ca for the most up-to-date information.

Get your free PDF filled with tools, tips, how-to's, as well as the do's and don'ts of effective political action. Learn how you can impact this election and what to do before the next one.

VoteGuns.ca/ShowUp

Newfoundland and Labrador

Avalon, Electoral District #10001

Recommended Vote to Keep Your Guns

Vote Conservative.

History at a Glance: 1st and 2nd Place

2004: Liberal over Conservative by 9,124 votes, 29% of votes cast.
2006: Conservative over Liberal by 4,814 votes, 13% of votes cast.
2008: Liberal over Conservative by 3,324 votes, 10% of votes cast.
2011: Liberal over Conservative by 1,259 votes, 3.5% of votes cast.
2015: Liberal over Conservative by 16,027 votes, 38% of votes cast.

Analysis

This riding voted Liberal in four of the past five elections, including Election 2015. Voter turnout rose from 57% in 2011 to 61% in 2015.

Bonavista–Burin–Trinity, Electoral District #10002

Recommended Vote to Keep Your Guns

Vote Conservative.

History at a Glance: 1st and 2nd Place

2004: Liberal over Conservative by 2,184 votes, 6.6% of votes cast.
2006: Liberal over Conservative by 4,490 votes, 12% of votes cast.
2008: Liberal over Conservative by 15,735 votes, 55% of votes cast.
2011: Liberal over Conservative by 9,382 votes, 30% of votes cast.
2015: Liberal over Conservative by 20,044 votes, 57% of votes cast.

Analysis

This riding tends to vote Liberal. Their candidates won the past five elections. Voter turnout rose from 45% in 2011 to 55% in 2015.

Coast of Bays–Central–Notre Dame, Electoral District #10003

Recommended Vote to Keep Your Guns

Vote Conservative.

History at a Glance: 1st and 2nd Place

2004: Liberal over Conservative by 11,282 votes, 40% of votes cast.
2006: Liberal over Conservative by 7,071 votes, 22% of votes cast.
2008: Liberal over NDP by 13,353 votes, 51% of votes cast.
2011: Liberal over Conservative by 9,560 votes, 32% of votes cast.
2015: Liberal over Conservative by 25,804 votes, 62% of votes cast.

Analysis

This riding tends to vote Liberal. Their candidates won the past five elections. Voter turnout rose from 51% in 2011 to 58% in 2015.

Labrador, Electoral District #10004

Recommended Vote to Keep Your Guns

Vote Conservative.

History at a Glance: 1st and 2nd Place

2004: Liberal over Conservative by 4,124 votes, 46% of votes cast.
2006: Liberal over Conservative by 1,240 votes, 11% of votes cast.
2008: Liberal over NDP by 4,048 votes, 52% of votes cast.
2011: Conservative over Liberal by 79 votes, 0.7% of votes cast.
2013 By-Election: Liberal over Conservative by 1,888 votes, 16% of votes cast.
2015: Liberal over NDP by 7,099 votes, 57% of votes cast.

Analysis

This riding tends to vote Liberal with their candidates winning five of the past six elections, including Election 2015. In Election 2015 this race was between the Liberal and the NDP candidates. Voter turnout rose from 53% in 2011 to 62% in 2015.

Long Range Mountains, Electoral District #10005

Recommended Vote to Keep Your Guns

Vote Conservative.

History at a Glance: 1st and 2nd Place

2004: Liberal over NDP by 3,586 votes, 14% of votes cast.
2006: Liberal over Conservative by 1,420 votes, 4.7% of votes cast.
2008: Liberal over NDP by 6,994 votes, 30% of votes cast.
2011: Liberal over Conservative by 4,592 votes, 18% of votes cast.
2015: Liberal over Conservative by 25,170 votes, 72% of votes cast.
2017 By-Election: Liberal over Conservative by 5,839 votes, 46% of votes cast.

Analysis

This riding tends to vote Liberal. Their candidates won the past five elections. Voter turnout rose from 45% in 2011 to 56% in 2015.

St. John's East, Electoral District #10006

Recommended Vote to Keep Your Guns

Vote NDP because they are your best choice to defeat the Liberals.

History at a Glance: 1st and 2nd Place

2004: Conservative over Liberal by 1,730 votes, 4.8% of votes cast.
2006: Conservative over Liberal by 4,765 votes, 12% of votes cast.
2008: NDP over Liberal by 25,670 votes, 62% of votes cast.
2011: NDP over Conservative by 22,190 votes, 50% of votes cast.
2015: Liberal over NDP by 646 votes, 1.4% of votes cast.

Analysis

Election 2015 was the first win for the Liberals in the past five elections. The NDP won the two elections prior to 2015.

Voter turnout rose from 58% in 2011 to 68% in 2015.

St. John's South–Mount Pearl, Electoral District #10007

Recommended Vote to Keep Your Guns

Vote NDP because they are your best choice to defeat the Liberals.

History at a Glance: 1st and 2nd Place

2004: Conservative over Liberal by 1,451 votes, 4.3% of votes cast.
2006: Conservative over Liberal by 4,349 votes, 12% of votes cast.
2008: Liberal over NDP by 949 votes, 2.8% of votes cast.
2011: NDP over Liberal by 7,551 votes, 19% of votes cast.
2015: Liberal over NDP by 9,455 votes, 21% of votes cast.

Analysis

This riding elected Liberal candidates in two of the past five elections, including Election 2015. The main battle here is between Liberal and NDP. Voter turnout rose from 58% in 2011 to 66% in 2015.

Prince Edward Island

Cardigan, Electoral District #11001

Recommended Vote to Keep Your Guns

Vote Conservative.

History at a Glance: 1st and 2nd Place

2004: Liberal over Conservative by 4,175 votes, 20% of votes cast.
2006: Liberal over Conservative by 4,619 votes, 22% of votes cast.
2008: Liberal over Conservative by 4,444 votes, 23% of votes cast.
2011: Liberal over Conservative by 2,379 votes, 11% of votes cast.
2015: Liberal over Conservative by 10,989 votes, 49% of votes cast.

Analysis

This riding tends to vote Liberal. Their candidates won the past five elections. Voter turnout rose from 77% in 2011 to 78% in 2015.

Charlottetown, Electoral District #11002

Recommended Vote to Keep Your Guns

Vote Conservative.

History at a Glance: 1st and 2nd Place

2004: Liberal over Conservative by 4,054 votes, 22% of votes cast.
2006: Liberal over Conservative by 3,062 votes, 16% of votes cast.
2008: Liberal over Conservative by 3,189 votes, 18% of votes cast.
2011: Liberal over Conservative by 1,252 votes, 6.8% of votes cast.
2015: Liberal over NDP by 7,013 votes, 33% of votes cast.

Analysis

This riding tends to vote Liberal. Their candidates won the past five elections and in Election 2015 this race was between the Liberal and NDP candidates. Voter turnout rose from 69% in 2011 to 75% in 2015.

Egmont, Electoral District #11003

Recommended Vote to Keep Your Guns

Vote Conservative.

History at a Glance: 1st and 2nd Place

2004: Liberal over Conservative by 4,857 votes, 26% of votes cast.
2006: Liberal over Conservative by 4,297 votes, 22% of votes cast.
2008: Conservative over Liberal by 55 votes, 0.3% of votes cast.
2011: Conservative over Liberal by 4,470 votes, 23% of votes cast.
2015: Liberal over Conservative by 4,336 votes, 20% of votes cast.

Analysis

This riding tends to vote Liberal. Their candidates won three of the past five elections, including Election 2015. Voter turnout rose from 70% in 2011 to 77% in 2015.

Malpeque, Electoral District #11004

Recommended Vote to Keep Your Guns

Vote Conservative.

History at a Glance: 1st and 2nd Place

2004: Liberal over Conservative by 3,656 votes, 19% of votes cast.
2006: Liberal over Conservative by 3,071 votes, 16% of votes cast.
2008: Liberal over Conservative by 924 votes, 4.9% of votes cast.
2011: Liberal over Conservative by 671 votes, 3.3% of votes cast.
2015: Liberal over Conservative by 10,003 votes, 45% of votes cast.

Analysis

This riding tends to vote Liberal. Their candidates won the past five elections but Conservative candidates have come close to defeating the Liberal incumbent in 2008 and 2011. Voter turnout rose from 75% in 2011 to 78% in 2015.

Nova Scotia

Cape Breton–Canso, Electoral District #12001

Recommended Vote to Keep Your Guns

Vote Conservative.

History at a Glance: 1st and 2nd Place

2004: Liberal over NDP by 10,942 votes, 29% of votes cast.
2006: Liberal over Conservative by 11,684 votes, 29% of votes cast.
2008: Liberal over Conservative by 8,923 votes, 25% of votes cast.
2011: Liberal over Conservative by 5,605 votes, 16% of votes cast.
2015: Liberal over Conservative by 25,749 votes, 60% of votes cast.

Analysis

This riding tends to vote Liberal. Their candidates won the past five elections. Voter turnout rose from 62% in 2011 to 71% in 2015. The Liberal incumbent will not run again in 2019.

Central Nova, Electoral District #12002

Recommended Vote to Keep Your Guns

Vote Conservative.

History at a Glance: 1st and 2nd Place

2004: Conservative over NDP by 5,906 votes, 16% of votes cast.
2006: Conservative over NDP by 3,273 votes, 7.8% of votes cast.
2008: Conservative over Green by 5,315 votes, 14% of votes cast.
2011: Conservative over NDP by 11,914 votes, 31% of votes cast.
2015: Liberal over Conservative by 14,419 votes, 33% of votes cast.

Analysis

Election 2015 was the first win for the Liberals in the past five elections. This riding tends to vote Conservative. Their candidates won four of the past five elections. Voter turnout rose from 66% in 2011 to 74% in 2015.

Cumberland–Colchester, Electoral District #12003

Recommended Vote to Keep Your Guns

Vote Conservative.

History at a Glance: 1st and 2nd Place

2004: Conservative over Liberal by 9,597 votes, 24% of votes cast.
2006: Conservative over Liberal by 12,140 votes, 28% of votes cast.
2008: Independent over NDP by 22,429 votes, 57% of votes cast.
2011: Conservative over NDP by 11,719 votes, 29% of votes cast.
2015: Liberal over Conservative by 17,270 votes, 37% of votes cast.

Analysis

Election 2015 was the first win for the Liberals in the past five elections. Voter turnout rose from 58% in 2011 to 71% in 2015.

The Liberal incumbent will not run again in 2019.

Dartmouth–Cole Harbour, Electoral District #12004

Recommended Vote to Keep Your Guns

Vote NDP because they are your best choice to defeat the Liberals.

History at a Glance: 1st and 2nd Place

2004: Liberal over NDP by 3,962 votes, 9.6% of votes cast.
2006: Liberal over NDP by 4,415 votes, 9.8% of votes cast.
2008: Liberal over NDP by 3,223 votes, 7.9% of votes cast.
2011: NDP over Liberal by 497 votes, 1.1% of votes cast.
2015: Liberal over NDP by 17,227 votes, 37% of votes cast.

Analysis

This riding tends to vote Liberal. Their candidates won four of the past five elections, including Election 2015. Voter turnout rose from 61% in 2011 to 71% in 2015.

Halifax, Electoral District #12005

Recommended Vote to Keep Your Guns

Vote NDP because they are your best choice to defeat the Liberals.

History at a Glance: 1st and 2nd Place

2004: NDP over Liberal by 1,074 votes, 2.4% of votes cast.
2006: NDP over Liberal by 7,983 votes, 16% of votes cast.
2008: NDP over Liberal by 6,794 votes, 15% of votes cast.
2011: NDP over Liberal by 11,953 votes, 26% of votes cast.
2015: Liberal over NDP by 17,650 votes, 34% of votes cast.

Analysis

Election 2015 was the first win for the Liberals in the past five elections. This riding tends to vote NDP, whose candidates won the four elections prior to 2015. Voter turnout rose from 63% in 2011 to 71% in 2015.

Electoral District #12006 Halifax West

Recommended Vote to Keep Your Guns

Vote Conservative.

History at a Glance: 1st and 2nd Place

2004: Liberal over NDP by 7,855 votes, 20% of votes cast.
2006: Liberal over NDP by 11,020 votes, 25% of votes cast.
2008: Liberal over NDP by 4,883 votes, 12% of votes cast.
2011: Liberal over Conservative by 2,448 votes, 5.4% of votes cast.
2015: Liberal over Conservative by 8,269 votes, 16% of votes cast.

Analysis

This riding tends to vote Liberal. Their candidates won the past five elections. Voter turnout rose from 62% in 2011 to 72% in 2015.

Kings–Hants, Electoral District #12007

Recommended Vote to Keep Your Guns

Vote Conservative.

History at a Glance: 1st and 2nd Place

2004: Liberal over Conservative by 6,211 votes, 16% of votes cast.
2006: Liberal over Conservative by 5,719 votes, 13% of votes cast.
2008: Liberal over Conservative by 6,795 votes, 18% of votes cast.
2011: Liberal over Conservative by 1,173 votes, 2.9% of votes cast.
2015: Liberal over Conservative by 24,349 votes, 52% of votes cast.

Analysis

This riding tends to vote Liberal. Their candidates won the past five elections but the Liberal incumbent resigned and will not run in 2019. Voter turnout rose from 61% in 2011 to 69% in 2015.

Sackville–Preston–Chezzetcook, Electoral District #12008

Recommended Vote to Keep Your Guns

Vote NDP because they are your best choice to defeat the Liberals.

History at a Glance: 1st and 2nd Place

2004: NDP over Liberal by 6,703 votes, 17% of votes cast.
2006: NDP over Liberal by 12,927 votes, 30% of votes cast.
2008: NDP over Conservative by 16,081 votes, 41% of votes cast.
2011: NDP over Conservative by 9,821 votes, 24% of votes cast.
2015: Liberal over NDP by 6,548 votes, 14% of votes cast.

Analysis

Election 2015 was the first win for the Liberals in the past five elections. This riding tends to vote NDP. Their candidates won the four elections prior to 2015. Voter turnout rose from 59% in 2011 to 71% in 2015.

South Shore–St. Margarets, Electoral District #12009

Recommended Vote to Keep Your Guns

Vote Conservative.

History at a Glance: 1st and 2nd Place

2004: Conservative over Liberal by 2,296 votes, 5.8% of votes cast.
2006: Conservative over NDP by 3,419 votes, 8.3% of votes cast.
2008: Conservative over NDP by 932 votes, 2.3% of votes cast.
2011: Conservative over NDP by 2,915 votes, 7.0% of votes cast.
2015: Liberal over Conservative by 18,140 votes, 34% of votes cast.

Analysis

Election 2015 was the first win for the Liberals in the past five elections. This riding tends to vote Conservative and their candidates have won four of the past five elections. Voter turnout rose from 62% in 2011 to 69% in 2015.

Sydney–Victoria, Electoral District #12010

Recommended Vote to Keep Your Guns

Vote NDP because they are your best choice to defeat the Liberals.

History at a Glance: 1st and 2nd Place

2004: Liberal over NDP by 9,087 votes, 24% of votes cast.
2006: Liberal over NDP by 8,759 votes, 22% of votes cast.
2008: Liberal over NDP by 8,744 votes, 25% of votes cast.
2011: Liberal over Conservative by 765 votes, 2.1% of votes cast.
2015: Liberal over NDP by 24,644 votes, 60% of votes cast.

Analysis

This riding tends to vote Liberal. They've won the past five elections and voter turnout rose from 61% in 2011 to 68% in 2015. The Conservative candidate narrowly lost this riding in 2011 and is a good bet for winning in 2019. Pay attention to local polls.

The Liberal incumbent will not run again in 2019.

West Nova, Electoral District #12011

Recommended Vote to Keep Your Guns

Vote Conservative.

History at a Glance: 1st and 2nd Place

2004: Liberal over Conservative by 4,134 votes, 9.6% of votes cast.
2006: Liberal over Conservative by 512 votes, 1.1% of votes cast.
2008: Conservative over Liberal by 1,632 votes, 3.9% of votes cast.
2011: Conservative over Liberal by 4,380 votes, 10% of votes cast.
2015: Liberal over Conservative by 16,720 votes, 37% of votes cast.

Analysis

This riding tends to vote Liberal. Their candidates won three of the past five elections, including Election 2015, when voter turnout rose from 63% in 2011 to 68%. The Liberal incumbent will not run again in 2019, so the door is open for the Conservative Party to win this seat back.

New Brunswick

Acadie–Bathurst, Electoral District #13001

Recommended Vote to Keep Your Guns

Vote NDP because they are your best choice to defeat the Liberals.

History at a Glance: 1st and 2nd Place

2004: NDP over Liberal by 9,405 votes, 21% of votes cast.
2006: NDP over Liberal by 9,691 votes, 19% of votes cast.
2008: NDP over Liberal by 15,999 votes, 36% of votes cast.
2011: NDP over Conservative by 24,611 votes, 53% of votes cast.
2015: Liberal over NDP by 5,766 votes, 11% of votes cast.

Analysis

Election 2015 was the first win for the Liberals in the past five elections. This riding tends to vote NDP, who won the four previous elections prior to 2015. Voter turnout rose from 69% in 2011 to 76% in 2015.

Beauséjour, Electoral District #13002

Recommended Vote to Keep Your Guns35065

Vote Conservative.

History at a Glance: 1st and 2nd Place

2004: Liberal over Conservative by 10,330 votes, 25% of votes cast.
2006: Liberal over Conservative by 7,093 votes, 15% of votes cast.
2008: Liberal over Conservative by 7,553 votes, 18% of votes cast.
2011: Liberal over Conservative by 2,588 votes, 5.8% of votes cast.
2015: Liberal over NDP by 28,525 votes, 54% of votes cast.

Analysis

This riding tends to vote Liberal. Their candidates won the past five elections. In Election 2015 this race was between the Liberal and the NDP candidates and voter turnout rose from 70% in 2011 to 79%.

Fredericton, Electoral District #13003

Recommended Vote to Keep Your Guns

Vote Conservative.

History at a Glance: 1st and 2nd Place

2004: Liberal over Conservative by 5,626 votes, 13% of votes cast.
2006: Liberal over Conservative by 3,357 votes, 7.1% of votes cast.
2008: Conservative over Liberal by 4,643 votes, 11% of votes cast.
2011: Conservative over NDP by 10,947 votes, 25% of votes cast.
2015: Liberal over Conservative by 9,736 votes, 21% of votes cast.

Analysis

This riding tends to vote Liberal. Their candidates won three of the past five elections, including Election 2015. Voter turnout rose from 64% in 2011 to 75% in 2015.

Fundy Royal, Electoral District #13004

Recommended Vote to Keep Your Guns

Vote Conservative.

History at a Glance: 1st and 2nd Place

2004: Conservative over Liberal by 3,362 votes, 10% of votes cast.
2006: Conservative over Liberal by 7,651 votes, 21% of votes cast.
2008: Conservative over NDP by 9,304 votes, 28% of votes cast.
2011: Conservative over NDP by 11,361 votes, 31% of votes cast.
2015: Liberal over Conservative by 1,775 votes, 3.8% of votes cast.

Analysis

Election 2015 was the first win for the Liberals in the past five elections. This riding tends to vote Conservative. Their candidates won four of the past five elections. Voter turnout rose from 64% in 2011 to 74% in 2015.

Madawaska–Restigouche, Electoral District #13005

Recommended Vote to Keep Your Guns

Vote Conservative.

History at a Glance: 1st and 2nd Place

2004: Liberal over NDP by 5,407 votes, 17% of votes cast.
2006: Liberal over Conservative by 885 votes, 2.4% of votes cast.
2008: Liberal over Conservative by 4,864 votes, 14% of votes cast.
2011: Conservative over Liberal by 1,915 votes, 5.5% of votes cast.
2015: Liberal over NDP by 11,108 votes, 30% of votes cast.

Analysis

This riding tends to vote Liberal. Their candidates won four of the past five elections, including Election 2015. Voter turnout rose from 69% in 2011 to 73% in 2015.

Miramichi–Grand Lake, Electoral District #13006

Recommended Vote to Keep Your Guns

Vote Conservative.

History at a Glance: 1st and 2nd Place

2004: Liberal over Conservative by 6,199 votes, 19% of votes cast.
2006: Liberal over Conservative by 2,710 votes, 8.2% of votes cast.
2008: Conservative over Liberal by 1,468 votes, 5.1% of votes cast.
2011: Conservative over NDP by 9,015 votes, 29% of votes cast.
2015: Liberal over Conservative by 4,726 votes, 13% of votes cast.

Analysis

This riding tends to vote Liberal. Their candidates won three of the past five elections, including Election 2015. The Conservatives placed second in three of the past five elections and won twice. Voter turnout rose from 71% in 2011 to 75% in 2015.

Moncton–Riverview–Dieppe, Electoral District #13007

Recommended Vote to Keep Your Guns

Vote Conservative.

History at a Glance: 1st and 2nd Place

2004: Liberal over Conservative by 15,263 votes, 36% of votes cast.
2006: Liberal over Conservative by 8,454 votes, 18% of votes cast.
2008: Liberal over Conservative by 1,500 votes, 3.3% of votes cast.
2011: Conservative over Liberal by 2,161 votes, 4.4% of votes cast.
2015: Liberal over Conservative by 18,886 votes, 36% of votes cast.

Analysis

This riding tends to vote Liberal with Conservative candidates placing second. Liberal candidates won four of the past five elections, including Election 2015. Voter turnout rose from 65% in 2011 to 72% in 2015.

New Brunswick Southwest, Electoral District #13008

Recommended Vote to Keep Your Guns

Vote Conservative.

History at a Glance: 1st and 2nd Place

2004: Conservative over Liberal by 6,637 votes, 22% of votes cast.
2006: Conservative over Liberal by 9,278 votes, 28% of votes cast.
2008: Conservative over Liberal by 11,611 votes, 39% of votes cast.
2011: Conservative over NDP by 10,653 votes, 33% of votes cast.
2015: Liberal over Conservative by 2,031 votes, 5.4% of votes cast.

Analysis

Election 2015 was the first win for the Liberals in the past five elections. This riding tends to vote Conservative and their candidates have won four of the past five elections. Voter turnout rose from 64% in 2011 to 73% in 2015.

Saint John–Rothesay, Electoral District #13009

Recommended Vote to Keep Your Guns

Vote Conservative.

History at a Glance: 1st and 2nd Place

2004: Liberal over Conservative by 3,513 votes, 9.7% of votes cast.
2006: Liberal over Conservative by 1,449 votes, 3.6% of votes cast.
2008: Conservative over Liberal by 497 votes, 1.4% of votes cast.
2011: Conservative over NDP by 7,074 votes, 19% of votes cast.
2015: Liberal over Conservative by 7,719 votes, 18% of votes cast.

Analysis

This riding tends to vote Liberal. Their candidates won three of the past five elections, including Election 2015. Voter turnout rose from 58% in 2011 to 69% in 2015.

Tobique–Mactaquac, Electoral District #13010

Recommended Vote to Keep Your Guns

Vote Conservative.

History at a Glance: 1st and 2nd Place

2004: Liberal over Conservative by 3,008 votes, 8.6% of votes cast.
2006: Conservative over Liberal by 336 votes, 0.9% of votes cast.
2008: Conservative over Liberal by 11,298 votes, 36% of votes cast.
2011: Conservative over NDP by 14,720 votes, 44% of votes cast.
2015: Liberal over Conservative by 3,684 votes, 9.6% of votes cast.

Analysis

This riding tends to vote Conservative. Their candidates won three of the past five elections. The Liberal incumbent will not seek re-election, which leaves the door open for the Conservative Party to win back this seat.

Voter turnout rose from 63% in 2011 to 71% in 2015.

Québec

Abitibi–Baie-James–Nunavik–Eeyou, Electoral District #24001

Recommended Vote to Keep Your Guns

Vote Conservative.

History at a Glance: 1st and 2nd Place

2004: Bloc Québécois over Liberal by 572 votes, 2.1% of votes cast.
2006: Bloc Québécois over Liberal by 7,228 votes, 24% of votes cast.
2008: Bloc Québécois over Conservative by 2,573 votes, 9.3% of votes.
2011: NDP over Conservative by 6,872 votes, 22% of votes cast.
2015: NDP over Liberal by 310 votes, 3.1% of votes cast.

Analysis

This riding voted Bloc Québécois until NDP Leader Jack Layton's 2011 Orange Crush altered Québéc's electoral landscape. The NDP has taken in the past two elections, in which they beat the Conservative candidate in 2011 and the Liberal candidate in 2015.

The NDP incumbent will not run again in 2019, however, potentially opening the door for another party to take this seat.

Voter turnout rose from 53% in 2011 to 55% in 2015.

Abitibi–Témiscamingue, Electoral District #24002

Recommended Vote to Keep Your Guns

Vote for NDP incumbent Christine Moore.

History at a Glance: 1st and 2nd Place

2004: Bloc Québécois over Liberal by 11,584 votes, 27% of votes cast.
2006: Bloc Québécois over Conservative by 14,003 votes, 30% of votes.
2008: Bloc Québécois over Liberal by 11,874 votes, 27% of votes cast.
2011: NDP over Bloc Québécois by 9,505 votes, 20% of votes cast.
2015: NDP over Liberal by 5,903 votes, 12% of votes cast.

Analysis

This riding tended to vote Bloc Québécois until NDP Leader Jack Layton's 2011 Orange Crush altered Québéc's electoral landscape. Voter turnout rose from 59% in 2011 to 60% in 2015.

Ahuntsic-Cartierville, Electoral District #24003

Recommended Vote to Keep Your Guns

Vote Bloc Québécois because they are your best choice to defeat the Liberals.

History at a Glance: 1st and 2nd Place

2004: Liberal over Bloc Québécois by 1,214 votes, 2.5% of votes cast.
2006: Bloc Québécois over Liberal by 834 votes, 1.7% of votes cast.
2008: Bloc Québécois over Liberal by 423 votes, 0.9% of votes cast.
2011: Bloc Québécois over NDP by 708 votes, 1.5% of votes cast.
2015: Liberal over Bloc Québécois by 9,342 votes, 17% of votes cast.

Analysis

This riding tends to vote Bloc Québécois as their candidates won three of the past five elections. Voter turnout rose from 64% in 2011 to 67% in 2015.

Alfred-Pellan, Electoral District #24004

Recommended Vote to Keep Your Guns

Vote NDP because they are your best choice to defeat the Liberals.

History at a Glance: 1st and 2nd Place

2004: Bloc Québécois over Liberal by 5,123 votes, 9.6% of votes cast.
2006: Bloc Québécois over Liberal by 8,298 votes, 15% of votes cast.
2008: Bloc Québécois over Liberal by 5,092 votes, 9.6% of votes cast.
2011: NDP over Bloc Québécois by 10,594 votes, 19% of votes cast.
2015: Liberal over NDP by 11,332 votes, 21% of votes cast.

Analysis

This riding tended to vote Bloc Québécois until NDP Leader Jack Layton's 2011 Orange Crush altered Québéc's electoral landscape. Voter turnout rose from 65% in 2011 to 70% in 2015.

Argenteuil–La Petite-Nation, Electoral District #24005

Recommended Vote to Keep Your Guns

Vote NDP because they are your best choice to defeat the Liberals.

History at a Glance: 1st and 2nd Place

2004: Bloc Québécois over Liberal by 15,014 votes, 30% of votes cast.
2006: Bloc Québécois over Conservative by 15,394 votes, 29% of votes.
2008: Bloc Québécois over Liberal by 16,471 votes, 30% of votes cast.
2011: NDP over Bloc Québécois by 8,922 votes, 15% of votes cast.
2015: Liberal over NDP by 9,443 votes, 18% of votes cast.

Analysis

This riding tended to vote Bloc Québécois until NDP Leader Jack Layton's 2011 Orange Crush altered Québéc's electoral landscape. Voter turnout rose from 60% in 2011 to 65% in 2015.

Avignon–La Mitis–Matane–Matapédia, Electoral District #24006

Recommended Vote to Keep Your Guns

Vote Bloc Québécois because they are your best choice to defeat the Liberals.

History at a Glance: 1st and 2nd Place

2004: Bloc Québécois over Liberal by 8,225 votes, 26% of votes cast.
2006: Bloc Québécois over Conservative by 5,564 votes, 16% of votes.
2008: Bloc Québécois over Liberal by 616 votes, 1.9% of votes cast.
2011: Bloc Québécois over Liberal by 3,669 votes, 10% of votes cast.
2015: Liberal over Bloc Québécois by 6,737 votes, 19% of votes cast.

Analysis

This riding tends to vote Bloc Québécois. Their candidates won four of the past five elections. Voter turnout rose from 59% in 2011 to 60% in 2015.

Beauce, Electoral District #24007

Recommended Vote to Keep Your Guns

Vote for Conservative Party candidate Richard Lehoux in 2019.

History at a Glance: 1st and 2nd Place

2004: Liberal over Bloc Québécois by 2,281 votes, 4.8% of votes cast.
2006: Conservative over Bloc Québécois by 25,918 votes, 47% of votes.
2008: Conservative over Bloc Québécois by 24,740 votes, 48% of votes.
2011: Conservative over NDP by 10,968 votes, 21% of votes cast.
2015: Conservative over Liberal by 20,468 votes, 37% of votes cast.

Analysis

The Conservatives have dominated this riding by a wide margin for the past four elections. Maxime Bernier, the leader of the People's Party of Canada, is running against Conservative candidate Richard Lehoux. Polls consistently project a Conservative victory.

Beauport–Côte-de-Beaupré–Île d'Orléans–Charlevoix, Electoral District #24020

Recommended Vote to Keep Your Guns

Vote for Conservative incumbent Sylvie Boucher.

History at a Glance: 1st and 2nd Place

2004: Bloc Québécois over Liberal by 16,853 votes, 40% of votes cast.
2006: Bloc Québécois over Conservative by 7,610 votes, 17% of votes.
2008: Bloc Québécois over Conservative by 9,279 votes, 22% of votes.
2011: NDP over Bloc Québécois by 1,176 votes, 2.5% of votes cast.
2015: Conservative over Liberal by 3,347 votes, 6.6% of votes cast.

Analysis

This riding tended to vote Bloc Québécois until NDP Leader Jack Layton's 2011 Orange Crush altered Québéc's electoral landscape. The Conservatives won in 2015 for the first time in five elections.

Voter turnout rose from 61% in 2011 to 66% in 2015.

Beauport–Limoilou, Electoral District #24008

Recommended Vote to Keep Your Guns

Vote for Conservative incumbent Alupa Clarke.

History at a Glance: 1st and 2nd Place

2004: Bloc Québécois over Liberal by 11,123 votes, 24% of votes cast.
2006: Conservative over Bloc Québécois by 820 votes, 1.7% of votes cast.
2008: Conservative over Bloc Québécois by 2,032 votes, 4.2% of votes.
2011: NDP over Conservative by 10,461 votes, 20% of votes cast.
2015: Conservative over NDP by 2,580 votes, 5.1% of votes cast.

Analysis

This riding tends to vote Conservative. Their candidates won three of the past five elections, including Election 2015. Voter turnout rose from 62% in 2011 to 64% in 2015.

Bécancour–Nicolet–Saurel, Electoral District #24009

Recommended Vote to Keep Your Guns

Vote for Bloc Québécois incumbent Louis Plamondon.

History at a Glance: 1st and 2nd Place

2004: Bloc Québécois over Liberal by 20,452 votes, 42% of votes cast.
2006: Bloc Québécois over Conservative by 16,154 votes, 33% of votes.
2008: Bloc Québécois over Conservative by 17,917 votes, 37% of votes.
2011: Bloc Québécois over NDP by 1,341 votes, 2.7% of votes cast.
2015: Bloc Québécois over Liberal by 8,205 votes, 16% of votes cast.

Analysis

This riding tends to vote Bloc Québécois. Their candidates won the past five elections. Voter turnout rose from 64% in 2011 to 66% in 2015.

Bellechasse–Les Etchemins–Lévis, Electoral District #24010

Recommended Vote to Keep Your Guns

Vote for Conservative incumbent Steven Blaney.

History at a Glance: 1st and 2nd Place

2004: Bloc Québécois over Liberal by 8,266 votes, 17% of votes cast.
2006: Conservative over Bloc Québécois by 9,717 votes, 17% of votes.
2008: Conservative over Bloc Québécois by 11,038 votes, 20% of votes.
2011: Conservative over NDP by 5,960 votes, 10% of votes cast.
2015: Conservative over Liberal by 18,911 votes, 30% of votes cast.

Analysis

This riding tends to vote Conservative. Their candidates won four of the past five elections, including Election 2015. Voter turnout rose from 65% in 2011 to 68% in 2015.

Beloeil–Chambly, Electoral District #24011

Recommended Vote to Keep Your Guns

Vote for NDP incumbent Matthew Dubé.

History at a Glance: 1st and 2nd Place

2004: Bloc Québécois over Liberal by 21,251 votes, 38% of votes cast.
2006: Bloc Québécois over Conservative by 21,000 votes, 34% of votes.
2008: Bloc Québécois over Liberal by 21,124 votes, 33% of votes cast.
2011: NDP over Bloc Québécois by 10,444 votes, 15% of votes cast.
2015: NDP over Liberal by 1,147 votes, 1.7% of votes cast.

Analysis

This riding tended to vote Bloc Québécois until NDP Leader Jack Layton's 2011 Orange Crush altered Québéc's electoral landscape. Voter turnout rose from 70% in 2011 to 73% in 2015.

Berthier–Maskinongé, Electoral District #24012

Recommended Vote to Keep Your Guns

Vote for NDP incumbent Ruth Ellen Brosseau.

History at a Glance: 1st and 2nd Place

2004: Bloc Québécois over Liberal by 18,234 votes, 37% of votes cast.
2006: Bloc Québécois over Conservative by 9,233 votes, 17% of votes.
2008: Bloc Québécois over Conservative by 12,867 votes, 24% of votes.
2011: NDP over Bloc Québécois by 5,735 votes, 10% of votes cast.
2015: NDP over Bloc Québécois by 8,905 votes, 16% of votes cast.

Analysis

This riding tends to vote Bloc Québécois but the NDP's Ruth Ellen Brosseau won the seat in 2011 despite not campaigning in the riding and vacationing in Las Vegas on Election Day. She has since proven to be one of the most conscientious MPs in the House of Commons. Voter turnout, from 62% in 2011 to 66% in 2015.

Bourassa, Electoral District #24015

Recommended Vote to Keep Your Guns

Vote Bloc Québécois because they are your best choice to defeat the Liberals.

History at a Glance: 1st and 2nd Place

2004: Liberal over Bloc Québécois by 5,133 votes, 12% of votes cast.
2006: Liberal over Bloc Québécois by 4,928 votes, 11% of votes cast.
2008: Liberal over Bloc Québécois by 9,724 votes, 24% of votes cast.
2011: Liberal over NDP by 3,280 votes, 8.6% of votes cast.
2013 By-Election: Liberal over NDP by 3,059 votes, or 16% of votes cast.
2015: Liberal over Bloc Québécois by 15,185 votes, 34% of votes cast.

Analysis

This riding tends to vote Liberal. Their candidates won the past six elections. Voter turnout rose from 54% in 2011 to 63% in 2015.

Brome–Missisquoi, Electoral District #24016

Recommended Vote to Keep Your Guns

Vote Conservative.

History at a Glance: 1st and 2nd Place

2004: Liberal over Bloc Québécois by 1,072 votes, 2.4% of votes cast.
2006: Bloc Québécois over Liberal by 5,027 votes, 10% of votes cast.
2008: Bloc Québécois over Liberal by 1,204 votes, 2.4% of votes cast.
2011: NDP over Liberal by 10,818 votes, 21% of votes cast.
2015: Liberal over NDP by 11,361 votes, 19% of votes cast.

Analysis

The Conservative candidate, Bruno Côté, founded the organization of Quebec municipalities to fight against the province's firearm registry.

The riding elected Liberal candidates in two of the past five elections, including Election 2015. The Liberal incumbent will not run in 2019, creating an opening for the Conservatives.

Brossard–Saint-Lambert, Electoral District #24017

Recommended Vote to Keep Your Guns

Vote NDP because they are your best choice to defeat the Liberals.

History at a Glance: 1st and 2nd Place

2004: Liberal over Bloc Québécois by 2,559 votes, 4.9% of votes cast.
2006: Bloc Québécois over Liberal by 1,243 votes, 2.2% of votes cast.
2008: Liberal over Bloc Québécois by 69 votes, 0.1% of votes cast.
2011: NDP over Liberal by 8,536 votes, 14% of votes cast.
2015: Liberal over NDP by 14,743 votes, 26% of votes cast.

Analysis

This riding tends to vote Liberal. Their candidates won three of the past five elections, including Election 2015. Voter turnout rose from 64% in 2011 to 68% in 2015.

Charlesbourg–Haute-Saint-Charles, Electoral District #24019

Recommended Vote to Keep Your Guns

Vote for Conservative incumbent Pierre Paul-Hus.

History at a Glance: 1st and 2nd Place

2004: Bloc Québécois over Liberal by 11,975 votes, 26% of votes cast.
2006: Conservative over Bloc Québécois by 1,372 votes, 2.8% of votes.
2008: Conservative over Bloc Québécois by 5,964 votes, 12% of votes.
2011: NDP over Conservative by 7,911 votes, 15% of votes cast.
2015: Conservative over Liberal by 11,083 votes, 19% of votes cast.

Analysis

This riding tends to vote Conservative. Their candidates won three of the past five elections, including Election 2015. Voter turnout rose from 65% in 2011 to 69% in 2015.

Châteauguay–Lacolle, Electoral District #24021

Recommended Vote to Keep Your Guns

Vote Bloc Québécois because they are your best choice to defeat the Liberals.

History at a Glance: 1st and 2nd Place

2004: Bloc Québécois over Liberal by 13,953 votes, 27% of votes cast.
2006: Bloc Québécois over Conservative by 17,055 votes, 31% of votes.
2008: Bloc Québécois over Liberal by 14,982 votes, 27% of votes cast.
2011: NDP over Bloc Québécois by 14,199 votes, 25% of votes cast.
2015: Liberal over Bloc Québécois by 7,630 votes, 15% of votes cast.

Analysis

This riding tended to vote Bloc Québécois until NDP Leader Jack Layton's 2011 Orange Crush altered Québéc's electoral landscape. Voter turnout rose from 63% in 2011 to 68% in 2015.

Chicoutimi–Le Fjord, Electoral District #24022

Recommended Vote to Keep Your Guns

Vote for Conservative incumbent Richard Martel.

History at a Glance: 1st and 2nd Place

2004: Bloc Québécois over Liberal by 863 votes, 1.9% of votes cast.
2006: Bloc Québécois over Liberal by 4,645 votes, 9.3% of votes cast.
2008: Bloc Québécois over Conservative by 3,057 votes, 6.4% of votes.
2011: NDP over Bloc Québécois by 4,755 votes, 9.3% of votes cast.
2015: Liberal over NDP by 600 votes, 1.4% of votes cast.
2018 By-Election: Conservative over Liberal by 5,556 votes, 26% of votes.

Analysis

This riding tended to vote Bloc Québécois until NDP Leader Jack Layton's 2011 Orange Crush altered Québéc's electoral landscape. The Liberals won in 2015 by 600 votes and lost the 2018 By-election by over 5,000 votes. Voter turnout rose from 64% in 2011 to 66% in 2015.

Compton–Stanstead, Electoral District #24023

Recommended Vote to Keep Your Guns

Vote NDP because they are your best choice to defeat the Liberals.

History at a Glance: 1st and 2nd Place

2004: Bloc Québécois over Liberal by 4,698 votes, 11% of votes cast.
2006: Bloc Québécois over Conservative by 9,185 votes, 18% of votes.
2008: Bloc Québécois over Liberal by 9,386 votes, 19% of votes cast.
2011: NDP over Bloc Québécois by 10,918 votes, 22% of votes cast.
2015: Liberal over NDP by 5,282 votes, 9.5% of votes cast.

Analysis

This riding tended to vote Bloc Québécois until NDP Leader Jack Layton's 2011 Orange Crush altered Québéc's electoral landscape. Voter turnout rose from 63% in 2011 to 68% in 2015.

Dorval–Lachine–LaSalle, Electoral District #24024

Recommended Vote to Keep Your Guns

Vote NDP because they are your best choice to defeat the Liberals.

History at a Glance: 1st and 2nd Place

2004: Liberal over Bloc Québécois by 13,816 votes.
2006: Liberal over Bloc Québécois by 10,850 votes.
2008: Liberal over Conservative by 12,446 votes.
2011: NDP over Liberal by 3,536 votes.
2015: Liberal over NDP by 18,205 votes.

Analysis

This riding tends to vote Liberal. Their candidates won four of the past five elections, including Election 2015. Voter turnout rose from 58% in 2011 to 64% in 2015.

Drummond, Electoral District #24025

Recommended Vote to Keep Your Guns

Vote for NDP incumbent François Choquette.

History at a Glance: 1st and 2nd Place

2004: Bloc Québécois over Liberal by 14,079 votes, 33% of votes cast.
2006: Bloc Québécois over Conservative by 12,441 votes, 27% of votes.
2008: Bloc Québécois over Conservative by 6,123 votes, 13% of votes.
2011: NDP over Bloc Québécois by 14,079 votes, 30% of votes cast.
2015: NDP over Liberal by 2,040 votes, 3.9% of votes cast.

Analysis

This riding tended to vote Bloc Québécois until NDP Leader Jack Layton's 2011 Orange Crush altered Québéc's electoral landscape. Voter turnout rose from 61% in 2011 to 64% in 2015.

Gaspésie–Les Îles-de-la-Madeleine, Electoral District #24026

Recommended Vote to Keep Your Guns

Vote NDP because they are your best choice to defeat the Liberals.

History at a Glance: 1st and 2nd Place

2004: Bloc Québécois over Liberal by 8,867 votes, 23% of votes cast.
2006: Bloc Québécois over Conservative by 4,331 votes, 10% of votes.
2008: Bloc Québécois over Liberal by 4,796 votes, 13% of votes cast.
2011: NDP over Bloc Québécois by 777 votes, 2.1% of votes cast.
2015: Liberal over NDP by 2,460 votes, 6.2% of votes cast.

Analysis

This riding tended to vote Bloc Québécois until NDP Leader Jack Layton's 2011 Orange Crush altered Québéc's electoral landscape. Voter turnout rose from 53% in 2011 to 60% in 2015.

Gatineau, Electoral District #24027

Recommended Vote to Keep Your Guns

Vote NDP because they are your best choice to defeat the Liberals.

History at a Glance: 1st and 2nd Place

2004: Liberal over Bloc Québécois by 830 votes, 1.8% of votes cast.
2006: Bloc Québécois over Liberal by 4,267 votes, 7.9% of votes cast.
2008: Bloc Québécois over NDP by 1,577 votes, 3.0% of votes cast.
2011: NDP over Bloc Québécois by 26,643 votes, 47% of votes cast.
2015: Liberal over NDP by 15,724 votes, 27% of votes cast.

Analysis

This riding elected Liberal candidates in two of the past five elections, including Election 2015. The main battle here is between Liberal and NDP. Voter turnout rose from 64% in 2011 to 69% in 2015.

Hochelaga, Electoral District #24028

Recommended Vote to Keep Your Guns

Vote NDP because they are your best choice to defeat the Liberals.

History at a Glance: 1st and 2nd Place

2004: Bloc Québécois over Liberal by 15,764 votes, 34% of votes cast.
2006: Bloc Québécois over Liberal by 17,638 votes, 38% of votes cast.
2008: Bloc Québécois over Liberal by 13,278 votes, 21% of votes cast.
2011: NDP over Bloc Québécois by 7,863 votes, 15% of votes cast.
2015: NDP over Liberal by 500 votes, 0.9% of votes cast.

Analysis

This riding tended to vote Bloc Québécois until NDP Leader Jack Layton's 2011 Orange Crush altered Québéc's electoral landscape. Voter turnout rose from 64% in 2011 to 64% in 2015.

NDP incumbent Marjolaine Boutin-Sweet will not seek re-election in 2019.

Honoré-Mercier, Electoral District #24029

Recommended Vote to Keep Your Guns

Vote NDP because they are your best choice to defeat the Liberals.

History at a Glance: 1st and 2nd Place

2004: Liberal over Bloc Québécois by 2,762 votes, 5.7% of votes cast.
2006: Liberal over Bloc Québécois by 1,743 votes, 3.4% of votes cast.
2008: Liberal over Bloc Québécois by 7,673 votes, 16% of votes cast.
2011: NDP over Liberal by 2,904 votes, 6.0% of votes cast.
2015: Liberal over NDP by 20,733 votes, 40% of votes cast.

Analysis

This riding tends to vote Liberal. Their candidates won four of the past five elections, including Election 2015. Voter turnout rose from 59% in 2011 to 65% in 2015.

Hull–Aylmer, Electoral District #24030

Recommended Vote to Keep Your Guns

Vote NDP because they are your best choice to defeat the Liberals.

History at a Glance: 1st and 2nd Place

2004: Liberal over Bloc Québécois by 4,509 votes, 9.4% of votes cast.
2006: Liberal over Bloc Québécois by 1,788 votes, 3.3% of votes cast.
2008: Liberal over Bloc Québécois by 8,125 votes, 15% of votes cast.
2011: NDP over Liberal by 23,143 votes, 39% of votes cast.
2015: Liberal over NDP by 11,006 votes, 15% of votes cast.

Analysis

This riding tends to vote Liberal. Their candidates won four of the past five elections, including Election 2015. Voter turnout soared from 65% in 2011 to 92% in 2015, a huge jump since Election 2011.

Joliette, Electoral District #24031

Recommended Vote to Keep Your Guns

Vote for Bloc Québécois incumbent Gabriel Ste-Marie.

History at a Glance: 1st and 2nd Place

2004: Bloc Québécois over Liberal by 19,686 votes, 41% of votes cast.
2006: Bloc Québécois over Conservative by 14,438 votes, 27% of votes.
2008: Bloc Québécois over Conservative by 18,500 votes, 35% of votes.
2011: NDP over Bloc Québécois by 8,246 votes, 14% of votes cast.
2015: Bloc Québécois over Liberal by 2,880 votes, 5.1% of votes cast.

Analysis

This riding tends to vote Bloc Québécois. Their candidates won three of the past five elections, including Election 2015. Voter turnout rose from 62% in 2011 to 66% in 2015.

Jonquière, Electoral District #24032

Recommended Vote to Keep Your Guns

Vote for NDP incumbent Karine Trudel.

History at a Glance: 1st and 2nd Place

2004: Bloc Québécois over Liberal by 11,838 votes, 26% of votes cast.
2006: Conservative over Bloc Québécois by 6,693 votes, 13% of votes.
2008: Conservative over Bloc Québécois by 7,604 votes, 15% of votes.
2011: NDP over Conservative by 4,331 votes, 8.2% of votes cast.
2015: NDP over Liberal by 339 votes, 0.7% of votes cast.

Analysis

Several political parties have won this riding in the past five elections. Currently, the NDP is the front-runner and should be supported. Voter turnout rose from 65% in 2011 to 66% in 2015.

La Pointe-de-l'Île, Electoral District #24033

Recommended Vote to Keep Your Guns

Vote for Bloc Québécois incumbent Mario Beaulieu.

History at a Glance: 1st and 2nd Place

2004: Bloc Québécois over Liberal by 20,120 votes, 44% of votes cast.
2006: Bloc Québécois over Conservative by 21,966 votes, 45% of votes.
2008: Bloc Québécois over Liberal by 18,573 votes, 40% of votes cast.
2011: NDP over Bloc Québécois by 7,558 votes, 16% of votes cast.
2015: Bloc Québécois over Liberal by 2,768 votes, 3.9% of votes cast.

Analysis

This riding tends to vote Bloc Québécois. Their candidates won four of the past five elections, including Election 2015. Voter turnout soared from 59% in 2011 to 84% in 2015.

La Prairie, Electoral District #24034

Recommended Vote to Keep Your Guns

Vote Bloc Québécois because they are your best choice to defeat the Liberals.

History at a Glance: 1st and 2nd Place

2015: Liberal over Bloc Québécois by 5,886 votes, 10% of votes cast.

Analysis

This electoral district was created prior to the 2015 federal election.

Lac-Saint-Jean, Electoral District #24035

Recommended Vote to Keep Your Guns

Vote Conservative.

History at a Glance: 1st and 2nd Place

2004: Bloc Québécois over Liberal by 12,591 votes, 36% of votes cast.
2006: Bloc Québécois over Conservative by 3,123 votes, 8.0% of votes.
2008: Conservative over Bloc Québécois by 1,436 votes, 3.9% of votes.
2011: Conservative over NDP by 7,256 votes, 18% of votes cast.
2015: Conservative over NDP by 2,658 votes, 4.8% of votes cast.
2017 By-Election: Liberal over Conservative by 4,732 votes, 15% of votes cast.

Analysis

This riding tends to vote Conservative. Their candidates won three of the past six elections, including Election 2015. Voter turnout rose from 63% in 2011 to 65% in 2015.

Lac-Saint-Louis, Electoral District #24036

Recommended Vote to Keep Your Guns

Vote Conservative.

History at a Glance: 1st and 2nd Place

2004: Liberal over Conservative by 26,040 votes, 52% of votes cast.
2006: Liberal over Conservative by 11,424 votes, 22% of votes cast.
2008: Liberal over Conservative by 11,757 votes, 23% of votes cast.
2011: Liberal over NDP by 2,204 votes, 4.1% of votes cast.
2015: Liberal over Conservative by 29,108 votes, 47% of votes cast.

Analysis

This riding tends to vote Liberal. Their candidates won the past five elections. Voter turnout rose from 66% in 2011 to 73% in 2015.

LaSalle–Émard–Verdun, Electoral District #24037

Recommended Vote to Keep Your Guns

Vote NDP because they are your best choice to defeat the Liberals.

History at a Glance: 1st and 2nd Place

2004: Liberal over Bloc Québécois by 11,805 votes, 26% of votes cast.
2006: Liberal over Bloc Québécois by 9,250 votes, 20% of votes cast.
2008: Liberal over Bloc Québécois by 6,842 votes, 16% of votes cast.
2011: NDP over Liberal by 6,519 votes, 16% of votes cast.
2015: Liberal over NDP by 8,037 votes, 15% of votes cast.

Analysis

This riding tends to vote Liberal. Their candidates won four of the past five elections, including Election 2015. In Election 2015 this race was between the Liberal and the NDP candidates. Voter turnout rose from 56% in 2011 to 64% in 2015.

Laurentides–Labelle, Electoral District #24038

Recommended Vote to Keep Your Guns

Vote NDP because they are your best choice to defeat the Liberals.

History at a Glance: 1st and 2nd Place

2004: Bloc Québécois over Liberal by 14,216 votes, 29% of votes cast.
2006: Bloc Québécois over Conservative by 17,551 votes, 33% of votes.
2008: Bloc Québécois over Liberal by 10,813 votes, 20% of votes cast.
2011: NDP over Bloc Québécois by 7,001 votes, 12% of votes cast.
2015: Liberal over Bloc Québécois by 1,485 votes, 2.4% of votes cast.

Analysis

This riding tended to vote Bloc Québécois until NDP Leader Jack Layton's 2011 Orange Crush altered Québéc's electoral landscape. Voter turnout rose from 61% in 2011 to 65% in 2015.

Laurier–Sainte-Marie, Electoral District #24039

Recommended Vote to Keep Your Guns

Vote NDP because they are your best choice to defeat the Liberals.

History at a Glance: 1st and 2nd Place

2004: Bloc Québécois over Liberal by 20,274 votes, 42% of votes cast.
2006: Bloc Québécois over NDP by 18,608 votes, 34% of votes cast.
2008: Bloc Québécois over Liberal by 15,305 votes, 35% of votes cast.
2011: NDP over Bloc Québécois by 5,382 votes, 7.3% of votes cast.
2015: NDP over Bloc Québécois by 5,230 votes, 8.3% of votes cast.

Analysis

This riding tended to vote Bloc Québécois until NDP Leader Jack Layton's 2011 Orange Crush altered Québéc's electoral landscape. Voter turnout dropped from 92% in 2011 to 74% in 2015.

The NDP incumbent will retire before the 2019 federal election.

Laval–Les Îles, Electoral District #24040

Recommended Vote to Keep Your Guns

Vote NDP because they are your best choice to defeat the Liberals.

History at a Glance: 1st and 2nd Place

2004: Liberal over Bloc Québécois by 5,388 votes, 11% of votes cast.
2006: Liberal over Bloc Québécois by 3,312 votes, 6.2% of votes cast.
2008: Liberal over Bloc Québécois by 9,027 votes, 17% of votes cast.
2011: NDP over Liberal by 14,595 votes, 27% of votes cast.
2015: Liberal over NDP by 15,147 votes, 28% of votes cast.

Analysis

This riding tends to vote Liberal. Their candidates won four of the past five elections, including Election 2015. Voter turnout rose from 58% in 2011 to 66% in 2015.

Longueuil–Charles-LeMoyne, Electoral District #24041

Recommended Vote to Keep Your Guns

Vote NDP because they are your best choice to defeat the Liberals.

History at a Glance: 1st and 2nd Place

2004: Bloc Québécois over Liberal by 5,370 votes, 12% of votes cast.
2006: Bloc Québécois over Liberal by 10,172 votes, 22% of votes cast.
2008: Bloc Québécois over Liberal by 3,963 votes, 9.1% of votes cast.
2011: NDP over Bloc Québécois by 7,352 votes, 17% of votes cast.
2015: Liberal over Bloc Québécois by 4,327 votes, 8.4% of votes cast.

Analysis

This riding tended to vote Bloc Québécois until NDP Leader Jack Layton's 2011 Orange Crush altered Québéc's electoral landscape. Voter turnout rose from 60% in 2011 to 62% in 2015.

Longueuil–Saint-Hubert, Electoral District #24043

Recommended Vote to Keep Your Guns

Vote Bloc Québécois because they are your best choice to defeat the Liberals.

History at a Glance: 1st and 2nd Place

2004: Bloc Québécois over Liberal by 17,110 votes, 35% of votes cast.
2006: Bloc Québécois over Conservative by 18,094 votes, 36% of votes.
2008: Bloc Québécois over Liberal by 12,198 votes, 24% of votes cast.
2011: NDP over Bloc Québécois by 12,938 votes, 25% of votes cast.
2015: NDP over Liberal by 703 votes, 1.2% of votes cast.

Analysis

The Bloc Québécois was polling in second place in late August after the NDP incumbent left to run for the Green Party, making this a riding to watch.

Sign up for e-mail updates and alerts: VoteGuns.ca

Louis-Hébert, Electoral District #24044

Recommended Vote to Keep Your Guns

Vote Conservative.

History at a Glance: 1st and 2nd Place

2004: Bloc Québécois over Liberal by 5,072 votes, 9.1% of votes cast.
2006: Conservative over Bloc Québécois by 231 votes, 0.4% of votes cast.
2008: Bloc Québécois over Conservative by 4,649 votes, 8.0% of votes.
2011: NDP over Bloc Québécois by 8,733 votes, 14% of votes cast.
2015: Liberal over Conservative by 4,727 votes, 7.7% of votes cast.

Analysis

Election 2015 was the first win for the Liberals in the past five elections. Voter turnout rose from 73% in 2011 to 76% in 2015.

Louis-Saint-Laurent, Electoral District #24045

Recommended Vote to Keep Your Guns

Vote for Conservative incumbent Gérard Deltell.

History at a Glance: 1st and 2nd Place

2004: Bloc Québécois over Conservative by 3,281 votes, 5.6% of votes.
2006: Conservative over Bloc Québécois by 16,609 votes, 33% of votes.
2008: Conservative over Bloc Québécois by 10,353 votes, 21% of votes.
2011: NDP over Conservative by 1,295 votes, 2.3% of votes cast.
2015: Conservative over Liberal by 18,785 votes, 29% of votes cast.

Analysis

This riding tends to vote Conservative. Their candidates won three of the past five elections, including Election 2015. Voter turnout rose from 65% in 2011 to 70% in 2015.

Lévis–Lotbinière, Electoral District #24042

Recommended Vote to Keep Your Guns

Vote for Conservative incumbent Jacques Gourde.

History at a Glance: 1st and 2nd Place

2004: Bloc Québécois over Conservative by 9,617 votes, 22% of votes.
2006: Conservative over Bloc Québécois by 12,834 votes, 25% of votes.
2008: Conservative over Bloc Québécois by 11,757 votes, 23% of votes.
2011: Conservative over NDP by 777 votes, 1.4% of votes cast.
2015: Conservative over Liberal by 17,795 votes, 28% of votes cast

Analysis

This riding tends to vote Conservative. Their candidates won four of the past five elections, including Election 2015. Voter turnout rose from 68% in 2011 to 72% in 2015.

Manicouagan, Electoral District #24046

Recommended Vote to Keep Your Guns

Vote for Bloc Québécois incumbent Marilène Gill.

History at a Glance: 1st and 2nd Place

2004: Bloc Québécois over Liberal by 10,943 votes, 34% of votes cast.
2006: Bloc Québécois over Conservative by 11,691 votes, 32% of votes.
2008: Bloc Québécois over Conservative by 6,898 votes, 22% of votes.
2011: NDP over Bloc Québécois by 5,942 votes, 18% of votes cast.
2015: Bloc Québécois over Liberal by 4,995 votes, 12% of votes cast.

Analysis

This riding tends to vote Bloc Québécois. Their candidates won four of the past five elections, including Election 2015. Voter turnout rose from 51% in 2011 to 56% in 2015.

Marc-Aurèle-Fortin, Electoral District #24065

Recommended Vote to Keep Your Guns

Vote NDP because they are your best choice to defeat the Liberals.

History at a Glance: 1st and 2nd Place

2004: Bloc Québécois over Liberal by 16,288 votes, 31% of votes cast.
2006: Bloc Québécois over Conservative by 16,540 votes, 31% of votes.
2008: Bloc Québécois over Liberal by 11,824 votes, 21% of votes cast.
2011: NDP over Bloc Québécois by 13,637 votes, 23% of votes cast.
2015: Liberal over NDP by 9,496 votes, 17% of votes cast.

Analysis

This riding tended to vote Bloc Québécois until NDP Leader Jack Layton's 2011 Orange Crush altered Québéc's electoral landscape. Voter turnout rose from 67% in 2011 to 71% in 2015.

Mirabel, Electoral District #24048

Recommended Vote to Keep Your Guns

Vote for Bloc Québécois incumbent Simon Marcil.

History at a Glance: 1st and 2nd Place

2015: Bloc Québécois over NDP by 837 votes, 1.4% of votes cast.

Analysis

This electoral district was created prior to the 2015 federal election.

Montarville, Electoral District #24049

Recommended Vote to Keep Your Guns

Vote Bloc Québécois because they are your best choice to defeat the Liberals.

History at a Glance: 1st and 2nd Place

2004: Bloc Québécois over Liberal by 12,593 votes, 25% of votes cast.
2006: Bloc Québécois over Conservative by 16,058 votes, 30% of votes.
2008: Bloc Québécois over Liberal by 12,012 votes, 23% of votes cast.
2011: NDP over Bloc Québécois by 8,977 votes, 16% of votes cast.
2015: Liberal over Bloc Québécois by 2,388 votes, 4.1% of votes cast.

Analysis

This riding tended to vote Bloc Québécois until NDP Leader Jack Layton's 2011 Orange Crush altered Québéc's electoral landscape. Voter turnout rose from 66% in 2011 to 77% in 2015.

Montcalm, Electoral District #24050

Recommended Vote to Keep Your Guns

Vote for Bloc Québécois incumbent Luc Thériault.

History at a Glance: 1st and 2nd Place

2004: Bloc Québécois over Liberal by 26,468 votes, 55% of votes cast.
2006: Bloc Québécois over Conservative by 24,157 votes, 43% of votes.
2008: Bloc Québécois over Liberal by 25,132 votes, 42% of votes cast.
2011: NDP over Bloc Québécois by 14,825 votes, 23% of votes cast.
2015: Bloc Québécois over Liberal by 4,921 votes, 9.3% of votes cast.

Analysis

This riding tends to vote Bloc Québécois. Their candidates won four of the past five elections, including Election 2015. Voter turnout rose from 60% in 2011 to 63% in 2015.

Montmagny–L'Islet–Kamouraska–Rivière-du-Loup, Electoral District #24051

Recommended Vote to Keep Your Guns

Vote for Conservative incumbent Bernard Généreux.

History at a Glance: 1st and 2nd Place

2004: Bloc Québécois over Liberal by 12,203 votes, 28% of votes cast.
2006: Bloc Québécois over Conservative by 12,588 votes, 27% of votes.
2008: Bloc Québécois over Conservative by 6,854 votes, 15% of votes.
2011: NDP over Conservative by 9 votes, 0.0% of votes cast.
2015: Conservative over Liberal by 272 votes, 0.6% of votes cast.

Analysis

This riding tends to vote Bloc Québécois but their political fortunes changed with NDP Leader Jack Layton's 2011 Orange Crush.

Bernard Généreux won Election 2015 for the Conservative Party by 272 votes. Voter turnout rose from 60% in 2011 to 63% in 2015.

Mount Royal, Electoral District #24052

Recommended Vote to Keep Your Guns

Vote Conservative.

History at a Glance: 1st and 2nd Place

2004: Liberal over Conservative by 25,399 votes, 67% of votes cast.
2006: Liberal over Conservative by 17,627 votes, 48% of votes cast.
2008: Liberal over Conservative by 10,026 votes, 28% of votes cast.
2011: Liberal over Conservative by 2,260 votes, 5.8% of votes cast.
2015: Liberal over Conservative by 5,986 votes, 12% of votes cast.

Analysis

This riding tends to vote Liberal. Voter turnout rose from 57% in 2011 to 65% in 2015.

Mégantic–L'Érable, Electoral District #24047

Recommended Vote to Keep Your Guns

Vote for Conservative incumbent Luc Berthold.

History at a Glance: 1st and 2nd Place

2004: Bloc Québécois over Liberal by 3,486 votes, 8.1% of votes cast.
2006: Conservative over Bloc Québécois by 8,140 votes, 17% of votes.
2008: Conservative over Bloc Québécois by 8,414 votes, 19% of votes.
2011: Conservative over NDP by 10,215 votes, 23% of votes cast.
2015: Conservative over Liberal by 3,441 votes, 7.3% of votes cast.

Analysis

This riding tends to vote Conservative. Their candidates won four of the past five elections, including Election 2015. Voter turnout rose from 64% in 2011 to 66% in 2015.

Notre-Dame-de-Grâce–Westmount, Electoral District #24053

Recommended Vote to Keep Your Guns

Vote NDP because they are your best choice to defeat the Liberals.

History at a Glance: 1st and 2nd Place

2004: Liberal over Bloc Québécois by 16,415 votes, 41% of votes cast.
2006: Liberal over Conservative by 11,589 votes, 28% of votes cast.
2008: Liberal over NDP by 9,137 votes, 24% of votes cast.
2011: Liberal over NDP by 642 votes, 1.6% of votes cast.
2015: Liberal over NDP by 18,526 votes, 36% of votes cast.

Analysis

This riding tends to vote Liberal. Their candidates won the past five elections. Voter turnout rose from 53% in 2011 to 65% in 2015.

Outremont, Electoral District #24054

Recommended Vote to Keep Your Guns

Vote NDP because they are your best choice to defeat the Liberals.

History at a Glance: 1st and 2nd Place

2004: Liberal over Bloc Québécois by 2,945 votes, 7.7% of votes cast.
2006: Liberal over Bloc Québécois by 2,504 votes, 6.5% of votes cast.
2008: NDP over Liberal by 2,343 votes, 6.5% of votes cast.
2011: NDP over Liberal by 12,702 votes, 33% of votes cast.
2015: NDP over Liberal by 4,645 votes, 11% of votes cast.
2019 By-Election: Liberal over NDP by 1,944 votes, or 13% of votes cast.

Analysis

The riding of the NDP's former leader, this riding tends to vote NDP even though it elected Liberals in two of the past five elections, including the 2019 by-election.

Voter turnout rose from 59% in 2011 to 61% in 2015.

Papineau, Electoral District #24055

Recommended Vote to Keep Your Guns

Vote NDP because they are your best choice to defeat the Liberals.

History at a Glance: 1st and 2nd Place

2004: Liberal over Bloc Québécois by 468 votes, 0.8% of votes cast.
2006: Bloc Québécois over Liberal by 990 votes, 2.3% of votes cast.
2008: Liberal over Bloc Québécois by 1,189 votes, 2.8% of votes cast.
2011: Liberal over NDP by 4,327 votes, 10% of votes cast.
2015: Liberal over NDP by 13,259 votes, 18% of votes cast.

Analysis

This riding, the current seat of Prime Minister Justin Trudeau, tends to vote Liberal. Their candidates won four of the past five elections, including Election 2015.

Voter turnout rose from 60% in 2011 to 65% in 2015.

Pierre-Boucher–Les Patriotes–Verchères, Electoral District #24014

Recommended Vote to Keep Your Guns

Vote for Bloc Québécois incumbent Xavier Barsalou-Duval.

History at a Glance: 1st and 2nd Place

2004: Bloc Québécois over Liberal by 23,375 votes, 47% of votes cast.
2006: Bloc Québécois over Conservative by 18,771 votes, 36% of votes.
2008: Bloc Québécois over Liberal by 18,731 votes, 35% of votes cast.
2011: NDP over Bloc Québécois by 3,921 votes, 6.9% of votes cast.
2015: Bloc Québécois over Liberal by 213 votes, 0.4% of votes cast.

Analysis

This riding tends to vote Bloc Québécois. Their candidates won four of the past five elections, including Election 2015. Voter turnout rose from 70% in 2011 to 75% in 2015.

Pierrefonds–Dollard, Electoral District #24056

Recommended Vote to Keep Your Guns

Vote NDP because they are your best choice to defeat the Liberals.

History at a Glance: 1st and 2nd Place

2004: Liberal over Bloc Québécois by 22,175 votes, 48% of votes cast.
2006: Liberal over Conservative by 13,375 votes, 28% of votes cast.
2008: Liberal over Conservative by 9,653 votes, 21% of votes cast.
2011: NDP over Liberal by 1,758 votes, 3.7% of votes cast.
2015: Liberal over Conservative by 22,625 votes, 39% of votes cast.

Analysis

This riding tends to vote Liberal. Their candidates won four of the past five elections, including Election 2015. Voter turnout rose from 59% in 2011 to 69% in 2015.

The Liberal incumbent will not seek re-election, opening the door for the NDP to retake this seat.

Pontiac, Electoral District #24057

Recommended Vote to Keep Your Guns

Vote NDP because they are your best choice to defeat the Liberals.

History at a Glance: 1st and 2nd Place

2004: Liberal over Bloc Québécois by 3,673 votes, 9.2% of votes cast.
2006: Conservative over Bloc Québécois by 2,371 votes, 5.0% of votes.
2008: Conservative over Liberal by 3,627 votes, 8.5% of votes cast.
2011: NDP over Conservative by 7,935 votes, 16% of votes cast.
2015: Liberal over NDP by 20,064 votes, 32% of votes cast.

Analysis

This riding elected Liberal candidates in two of the past five elections, including Election 2015. The main battle here is between Liberal and NDP. Voter turnout rose from 59% in 2011 to 71% in 2015.

Portneuf–Jacques-Cartier, Electoral District #24058

Recommended Vote to Keep Your Guns

Vote for Conservative incumbent Joël Godin.

History at a Glance: 1st and 2nd Place

2004: Bloc Québécois over Liberal by 6,608 votes, 15% of votes cast.
2006: Independent over Bloc Québécois by 7,064 votes, 14% of votes.
2008: Independent over Bloc Québécois by 662 votes, 1.5% of votes cast.
2011: NDP over Independent by 7,793 votes, 15% of votes cast.
2015: Conservative over NDP by 13,604 votes, 22% of votes cast.

Analysis

In 2006, voters elected right-of-center radio host André Arthur. He was re-elected in 2008, but lost to the NDP's Orange Crush in 2011.

In 2015, voters returned to their right-of-center roots and elected Conservative candidate Joël Godin.

Voter turnout rose from 65% in 2011 to 70% in 2015.

Québec, Electoral District #24059

Recommended Vote to Keep Your Guns

Vote NDP because they are your best choice to defeat the Liberals.

History at a Glance: 1st and 2nd Place

2004: Bloc Québécois over Liberal by 11,391 votes, 24% of votes cast.
2006: Bloc Québécois over Conservative by 5,902 votes, 12% of votes.
2008: Bloc Québécois over Conservative by 8,121 votes, 16% of votes.
2011: NDP over Bloc Québécois by 7,709 votes, 15% of votes cast.
2015: Liberal over NDP by 1,000 votes, 1.9% of votes cast.

Analysis

This riding tended to vote Bloc Québécois until NDP Leader Jack Layton's 2011 Orange Crush altered Québéc's electoral landscape. Voter turnout rose from 65% in 2011 to 68% in 2015.

Repentigny, Electoral District #24060

Recommended Vote to Keep Your Guns

Vote for Bloc Québécois incumbent Monique Pauzé.

History at a Glance: 1st and 2nd Place

2004: Bloc Québécois over Liberal by 26,554 votes, 52% of votes cast.
2006: Bloc Québécois over Conservative by 24,834 votes, 44% of votes.
2008: Bloc Québécois over NDP by 22,154 votes, 38% of votes cast.
2011: NDP over Bloc Québécois by 12,889 votes, 21% of votes cast.
2015: Bloc Québécois over Liberal by 4,820 votes, 7.4% of votes cast.

Analysis

This riding tends to vote Bloc Québécois. Their candidates won four of the past five elections, including Election 2015. Voter turnout rose from 66% in 2011 to 71% in 2015.

Richmond–Arthabaska, Electoral District #24061

Recommended Vote to Keep Your Guns

Vote for Conservative incumbent Alain Rayes.

History at a Glance: 1st and 2nd Place

2004: Bloc Québécois over Liberal by 13,402 votes, 28% of votes cast.
2006: Bloc Québécois over Conservative by 8,001 votes, 16% of votes.
2008: Bloc Québécois over Conservative by 8,833 votes, 17% of votes.
2011: Bloc Québécois over NDP by 717 votes, 1.3% of votes cast.
2015: Conservative over Liberal by 4,042 votes, 6.9% of votes cast.

Analysis

This riding tends to vote Bloc Québécois. Their candidates won four of the past five elections. Voter turnout rose from 65% in 2011 to 68% in 2015.

Rimouski-Neigette–Témiscouata–Les Basques, Electoral District #24018

Recommended Vote to Keep Your Guns

Vote for NDP incumbent Guy Caron.

History at a Glance: 1st and 2nd Place

2004: Bloc Québécois over Liberal by 13,054 votes, 34% of votes cast.
2006: Bloc Québécois over Conservative by 10,323 votes, 24% of votes.
2008: Bloc Québécois over Liberal by 9,715 votes, 25% of votes cast.
2011: NDP over Bloc Québécois by 5,190 votes, 12% of votes cast.
2015: NDP over Liberal by 6,780 votes, 15% of votes cast.

Analysis

This riding tended to vote Bloc Québécois until NDP Leader Jack Layton's 2011 Orange Crush altered Québéc's electoral landscape. Voter turnout rose from 62% in 2011 to 64% in 2015.

Rivière-des-Mille-Îles, Electoral District #24062

Recommended Vote to Keep Your Guns

Vote NDP because they are your best choice to defeat the Liberals.

History at a Glance: 1st and 2nd Place

2004: Bloc Québécois over Liberal by 16,968 votes, 37% of votes cast.
2006: Bloc Québécois over Conservative by 16,099 votes, 33% of votes.
2008: Bloc Québécois over Conservative by 13,305 votes, 26% of votes.
2011: NDP over Bloc Québécois by 10,766 votes, 21% of votes cast.
2015: Liberal over NDP by 1,676 votes, 2.9% of votes cast.

Analysis

Election 2015 was the first win for the Liberals in the past five elections. This riding tended to vote Bloc Québécois until NDP Leader Jack Layton's 2011 Orange Crush altered Québéc's electoral landscape. Voter turnout rose from 65% in 2011 to 71% in 2015.

Rivière-du-Nord, Electoral District #24063

Recommended Vote to Keep Your Guns

Vote for Bloc Québécois incumbent Rhéal Fortin.

History at a Glance: 1st and 2nd Place

2004: Bloc Québécois over Liberal by 19,695 votes, 45% of votes cast.
2006: Bloc Québécois over Conservative by 18,020 votes, 38% of votes.
2008: Bloc Québécois over NDP by 19,401 votes, 39% of votes cast.
2011: NDP over Bloc Québécois by 14,498 votes, 27% of votes cast.
2015: Bloc Québécois over NDP by 1,080 votes, 1.9% of votes cast.

Analysis

This riding tends to vote Bloc Québécois. Their candidates won four of the past five elections, including Election 2015. Voter turnout rose from 59% in 2011 to 63% in 2015.

Rosemont–La Petite-Patrie, Electoral District #24064

Recommended Vote to Keep Your Guns

Vote for NDP incumbent Alexandre Boulerice.

History at a Glance: 1st and 2nd Place

2004: Bloc Québécois over Liberal by 19,652 votes, 39% of votes cast.
2006: Bloc Québécois over Liberal by 21,077 votes, 40% of votes cast.
2008: Bloc Québécois over Liberal by 17,475 votes, 28% of votes cast.
2011: NDP over Bloc Québécois by 9,782 votes, 18% of votes cast.
2015: NDP over Bloc Québécois by 16,389 votes, 27% of votes cast.

Analysis

This riding tended to vote Bloc Québécois until NDP Leader Jack Layton's 2011 Orange Crush altered Québéc's electoral landscape. Voter turnout rose from 66% in 2011 to 71% in 2015.

Saint-Hyacinthe–Bagot, Electoral District #24066

Recommended Vote to Keep Your Guns

Vote for NDP incumbent Brigitte Sansoucy.

History at a Glance: 1st and 2nd Place

2004: Bloc Québécois over Liberal by 19,231 votes, 40% of votes cast.
2006: Bloc Québécois over Conservative by 15,515 votes, 31% of votes.
2008: Bloc Québécois over Conservative by 12,524 votes, 26% of votes.
2011: NDP over Bloc Québécois by 14,312 votes, 28% of votes cast.
2015: NDP over Liberal by 598 votes, 1.1% of votes cast.

Analysis

This riding tended to vote Bloc Québécois until NDP Leader Jack Layton's 2011 Orange Crush altered Québéc's electoral landscape.

Voter turnout rose from 65% in 2011 to 67% in 2015.

Saint-Jean, Electoral District #24067

Recommended Vote to Keep Your Guns

Vote NDP because they are your best choice to defeat the Liberals.

History at a Glance: 1st and 2nd Place

2004: Bloc Québécois over Liberal by 16,756 votes, 34% of votes cast.
2006: Bloc Québécois over Conservative by 16,554 votes, 32% of votes.
2008: Bloc Québécois over Liberal by 17,076 votes, 32% of votes cast.
2011: NDP over Bloc Québécois by 8,920 votes, 17% of votes cast.
2015: Liberal over NDP by 2,467 votes, 4.1% of votes cast.

Analysis

This riding tended to vote Bloc Québécois until NDP Leader Jack Layton's 2011 Orange Crush altered Québéc's electoral landscape. Voter turnout rose from 61% in 2011 to 68% in 2015.

Saint-Laurent, Electoral District #24068

Recommended Vote to Keep Your Guns

Vote NDP because they are your best choice to defeat the Liberals.

History at a Glance: 1st and 2nd Place

2004: Liberal over Bloc Québécois by 20,846 votes, 47% of votes cast.
2006: Liberal over Bloc Québécois by 19,220 votes, 45% of votes cast.
2008: Liberal over Conservative by 18,096 votes, 45% of votes cast.
2011: Liberal over NDP by 5,778 votes, 14% of votes cast.
2015: Liberal over Conservative by 16,965 votes, 42% of votes cast.
2017 By-Election: Liberal over Conservative by 7,677 votes, or 40% of votes cast.

Analysis

This riding tends to vote Liberal. Their candidates won the past five elections. Voter turnout rose from 52% in 2011 to 58% in 2015.

Saint-Léonard–Saint-Michel, Electoral District #24069

Recommended Vote to Keep Your Guns

Vote NDP because they are your best choice to defeat the Liberals.

History at a Glance: 1st and 2nd Place

2004: Liberal over Bloc Québécois by 17,032 votes, 42% of votes cast.
2006: Liberal over Bloc Québécois by 15,933 votes, 38% of votes cast.
2008: Liberal over Conservative by 16,025 votes, 42% of votes cast.
2011: Liberal over NDP by 3,620 votes, 10.0% of votes cast.
2015: Liberal over NDP by 22,215 votes, 50% of votes cast.

Analysis

This riding tends to vote Liberal. Their candidates won the past five elections. Voter turnout rose from 50% in 2011 to 58% in 2015.

The one-term Liberal incumbent will not run in 2019.

Saint-Maurice–Champlain, Electoral District #24070

Recommended Vote to Keep Your Guns

Vote NDP because they are your best choice to defeat the Liberals.

History at a Glance: 1st and 2nd Place

2004: Bloc Québécois over Liberal by 11,598 votes, 25% of votes cast.
2006: Bloc Québécois over Conservative by 5,504 votes, 11% of votes.
2008: Bloc Québécois over Conservative by 9,314 votes, 20% of votes.
2011: NDP over Bloc Québécois by 4,667 votes, 9.8% of votes cast.
2015: Liberal over NDP by 12,230 votes, 21% of votes cast.

Analysis

This riding tended to vote Bloc Québécois until NDP Leader Jack Layton's 2011 Orange Crush altered Québéc's electoral landscape. Voter turnout rose from 59% in 2011 to 64% in 2015.

Salaberry–Suroît, Electoral District #24071

Recommended Vote to Keep Your Guns

Vote NDP because they are your best choice to defeat the Liberals.

History at a Glance: 1st and 2nd Place

2004: Bloc Québécois over Liberal by 8,482 votes, 16% of votes cast.
2006: Bloc Québécois over Conservative by 11,581 votes, 21% of votes.
2008: Bloc Québécois over Conservative by 16,046 votes, 30% of votes.
2011: NDP over Bloc Québécois by 5,816 votes, 11% of votes cast.
2015: NDP over Liberal by 771 votes, 1.3% of votes cast.

Analysis

This riding tended to vote Bloc Québécois until NDP Leader Jack Layton's 2011 Orange Crush altered Québéc's electoral landscape. The NDP incumbent will not run again in 2019.

Voter turnout rose from 61% in 2011 to 66% in 2015.

Shefford, Electoral District #24072

Recommended Vote to Keep Your Guns

Vote Conservative.

History at a Glance: 1st and 2nd Place

2004: Bloc Québécois over Liberal by 3,243 votes, 6.9% of votes cast.
2006: Bloc Québécois over Conservative by 9,425 votes, 18% of votes.
2008: Bloc Québécois over Liberal by 10,840 votes, 21% of votes cast.
2011: NDP over Bloc Québécois by 14,960 votes, 28% of votes cast.
2015: Liberal over NDP by 9,012 votes, 15% of votes cast.

Analysis

This riding tends to vote Bloc Québécois but their political fortunes changed with NDP Leader Jack Layton's 2011 Orange Crush.

Voter turnout rose from 64% in 2011 to 67% in 2015.

Sherbrooke, Electoral District #24073

Recommended Vote to Keep Your Guns

Vote for NDP incumbent Pierre-Luc Dusseault.

History at a Glance: 1st and 2nd Place

2004: Bloc Québécois over Liberal by 13,841 votes, 28% of votes cast.
2006: Bloc Québécois over Conservative by 16,349 votes, 31% of votes.
2008: Bloc Québécois over Liberal by 15,555 votes, 31% of votes cast.
2011: NDP over Bloc Québécois by 3,750 votes, 7.2% of votes cast.
2015: NDP over Liberal by 4,339 votes, 7.6% of votes cast.

Analysis

This riding tended to vote Bloc Québécois until NDP Leader Jack Layton's 2011 Orange Crush altered Québéc's electoral landscape. NDP incumbent Pierre-Luc Dusseault won in Election 2015. Voter turnout rose from 63% in 2011 to 65% in 2015.

Terrebonne, Electoral District #24075

Recommended Vote to Keep Your Guns

Vote for Bloc Québécois incumbent Michel Boudrias.

History at a Glance: 1st and 2nd Place

2004: Bloc Québécois over Liberal by 22,240 votes, 48% of votes cast.
2006: Bloc Québécois over Conservative by 19,985 votes, 39% of votes.
2008: Bloc Québécois over Liberal by 19,366 votes, 36% of votes cast.
2011: NDP over Bloc Québécois by 10,597 votes, 19% of votes cast.
2015: Bloc Québécois over Liberal by 2,922 votes, 5.0% of votes cast.

Analysis

This riding tends to vote Bloc Québécois. Their candidates won four of the past five elections, including Election 2015. Voter turnout rose from 65% in 2011 to 69% in 2015.

Thérèse-De Blainville, Electoral District #24013

Recommended Vote to Keep Your Guns

Vote Bloc Québécois because they are your best choice to defeat the Liberals.

History at a Glance: 1st and 2nd Place

2015: Liberal over Bloc Québécois by 3,043 votes, 5.4% of votes cast.

Analysis

This electoral district was created prior to the 2015 federal election.

Trois-Rivières, Electoral District #24076

Recommended Vote to Keep Your Guns

Vote for NDP incumbent Robert Aubin.

History at a Glance: 1st and 2nd Place

2004: Bloc Québécois over Liberal by 13,537 votes, 29% of votes cast.
2006: Bloc Québécois over by 6,908 votes, 14% of votes cast.
2008: Bloc Québécois over Conservative by 10,407 votes, 21% of votes.
2011: NDP over Bloc Québécois by 14,994 votes, 30% of votes cast.
2015: NDP over Liberal by 969 votes, 1.6% of votes cast.

Analysis

This riding tended to vote Bloc Québécois until NDP Leader Jack Layton's 2011 Orange Crush altered Québéc's electoral landscape. Voter turnout rose from 63% in 2011 to 66% in 2015.

Vaudreuil–Soulanges, Electoral District #24074

Recommended Vote to Keep Your Guns

Vote NDP because they are your best choice to defeat the Liberals.

History at a Glance: 1st and 2nd Place

2004: Bloc Québécois over Liberal by 3,062 votes, 5.5% of votes cast.
2006: Bloc Québécois over Liberal by 9,151 votes, 15% of votes cast.
2008: Bloc Québécois over Conservative by 11,548 votes, 18% of votes.
2011: NDP over Bloc Québécois by 12,396 votes, 18% of votes cast.
2015: Liberal over NDP by 15,923 votes, 24% of votes cast.

Analysis

This riding tended to vote Bloc Québécois until NDP Leader Jack Layton's 2011 Orange Crush altered Québéc's electoral landscape. Voter turnout rose from 66% in 2011 to 72% in 2015.

Ville-Marie–Le Sud-Ouest–Île-des-Soeurs, Electoral District #24077

Recommended Vote to Keep Your Guns

Vote NDP because they are your best choice to defeat the Liberals.

History at a Glance: 1st and 2nd Place

2004: Liberal over Bloc Québécois by 72 votes, 0.2% of votes cast.
2006: Bloc Québécois over Liberal by 3,095 votes, 6.2% of votes cast.
2008: Bloc Québécois over Liberal by 1,303 votes, 2.7% of votes cast.
2011: NDP over Bloc Québécois by 10,658 votes, 20% of votes cast.
2015: Liberal over NDP by 13,734 votes, 27% of votes cast.

Analysis

This riding elected Liberal candidates in two of the past five elections, including Election 2015, when voter turnout rose from 58% in 2011 to 59%.

Vimy, Electoral District #24078

Recommended Vote to Keep Your Guns

Vote NDP because they are your best choice to defeat the Liberals.

History at a Glance: 1st and 2nd Place

2004: Bloc Québécois over Liberal by 6,786 votes, 14% of votes cast.
2006: Bloc Québécois over Liberal by 9,334 votes, 19% of votes cast.
2008: Bloc Québécois over Liberal by 4,895 votes, 9.7% of votes cast.
2011: NDP over Bloc Québécois by 10,483 votes, 21% of votes cast.
2015: Liberal over NDP by 13,691 votes, 25% of votes cast.

Analysis

This riding tended to vote Bloc Québécois until NDP Leader Jack Layton's 2011 Orange Crush altered Québéc's electoral landscape. Voter turnout rose from 60% in 2011 to 63% in 2015.

The first-term Liberal incumbent will not seek re-election.

Ontario

Ajax, Electoral District #35001

Recommended Vote to Keep Your Guns

Vote Conservative.

History at a Glance: 1st and 2nd Place

2004: Liberal over Conservative by 7,040 votes, 16% of votes cast.
2006: Liberal over Conservative by 8,644 votes, 17% of votes cast.
2008: Liberal over Conservative by 3,204 votes, 6.6% of votes cast.
2011: Conservative over Liberal by 3,228 votes, 5.7% of votes cast.
2015: Liberal over Conservative by 12,084 votes, 21% of votes cast.

Analysis

In 2011, Conservatives defeated the Liberal incumbent who works against gun owners. Election 2019 could be a repeat. Voter turnout rose from 60% in 2011 to 66% in 2015.

Algoma–Manitoulin–Kapuskasing, Electoral District #35002

Recommended Vote to Keep Your Guns

Vote for NDP incumbent Carol Hughes.

History at a Glance: 1st and 2nd Place

2004: Liberal over NDP by 3,225 votes, 9.2% of votes cast.
2006: Liberal over NDP by 1,408 votes, 3.7% of votes cast.
2008: NDP over Liberal by 4,347 votes, 13% of votes cast.
2011: NDP over Conservative by 7,756 votes, 21% of votes cast.
2015: NDP over Liberal by 2,405 votes, 5.8% of votes cast.

Analysis

This riding elected Liberal candidates in two of the past five elections and the primary battle is between Liberal and NDP. Voter turnout rose

Aurora–Oak Ridges–Richmond Hill, Electoral District #35003

Recommended Vote to Keep Your Guns

Vote for Conservative incumbent Leona Alleslev.

History at a Glance: 1st and 2nd Place

2015: Liberal over Conservative by 1,093 votes, 2.1% of votes cast.

Analysis

This electoral district was created prior to the 2015 federal election. After winning the election as a Liberal, Leona Alleslev switched parties and joined the Conservatives.

Barrie–Innisfil, Electoral District #35004

Recommended Vote to Keep Your Guns

Vote for Conservative incumbent John Brassard.

History at a Glance: 1st and 2nd Place

2004: Liberal over Conservative by 1,295 votes, 2.6% of votes cast.
2006: Conservative over Liberal by 1,543 votes, 2.7% of votes cast.
2008: Conservative over Liberal by 15,195 votes, 28% of votes cast.
2011: Conservative over NDP by 20,279 votes, 36% of votes cast.
2015: Conservative over Liberal by 4,593 votes, 9.3% of votes cast.

Analysis

This riding tends to vote Conservative. Their candidates won four of the past five elections, including Election 2015. Voter turnout rose from 60% in 2011 to 64% in 2015.

Barrie–Springwater–Oro-Medonte, Electoral District #35005

Recommended Vote to Keep Your Guns

Vote for Conservative incumbent Alex Nuttall.

History at a Glance: 1st and 2nd Place

2015: Conservative over Liberal by 86 votes, 0.2% of votes cast.

Analysis

This electoral district was created prior to the 2015 federal election but voters in this area typically support Conservative candidates.

Bay of Quinte, Electoral District #35006

Recommended Vote to Keep Your Guns

Vote Conservative.

History at a Glance: 1st and 2nd Place

2004: Conservative over Liberal by 2,419 votes, 4.5% of votes cast.
2006: Conservative over Liberal by 9,510 votes, 17% of votes cast.
2008: Conservative over Liberal by 12,013 votes, 23% of votes cast.
2011: Conservative over NDP by 16,122 votes, 30% of votes cast.
2015: Liberal over Conservative by 9,500 votes, 16% of votes cast.

Analysis

This riding typically votes Conservative. Election 2015 was the first win for the Liberals in the past five elections. Voter turnout, from 61% in 2011 to 68% in 2015.

Beaches–East York, Electoral District #35007

Recommended Vote to Keep Your Guns

Vote NDP because they are your best choice to defeat the Liberals.

2004: Liberal over NDP by 7,338 votes, 12% of votes cast.

2004: Liberal over NDP by 7,338 votes, 12% of votes cast.
2006: Liberal over NDP by 2,778 votes, 5.4% of votes cast.
2008: Liberal over NDP by 4,092 votes, 8.8% of votes cast.
2011: NDP over Liberal by 5,298 votes, 11% of votes cast.
2015: Liberal over NDP by 10,345 votes, 19% of votes cast.

Analysis

This riding typically votes Liberal. Their candidates won four of the past five elections, including Election 2015. Voter turnout rose from 66% in 2011 to 72% in 2015.

Brampton Centre, Electoral District #35008

Recommended Vote to Keep Your Guns

Vote Conservative.

History at a Glance: 1st and 2nd Place

2015: Liberal over Conservative by 5,932 votes, 15% of votes cast.

Analysis

This electoral district was created prior to the 2015 federal election and voters in this area typically support Liberal candidates.

Brampton East, Electoral District #35009

Recommended Vote to Keep Your Guns

Vote Conservative.

History at a Glance: 1st and 2nd Place

2004: Liberal over Conservative by 7,800 votes, 19% of votes cast.
2006: Liberal over Conservative by 8,981 votes, 18% of votes cast.
2008: Liberal over Conservative by 3,919 votes, 7.9% of votes cast.
2011: Conservative over NDP by 539 votes, 0.9% of votes cast.
2015: Liberal over Conservative by 13,010 votes, 29% of votes cast.

Analysis

This riding typically votes Liberal. Their candidates won four of the past five elections, including Election 2015. Voter turnout rose from 53% in 2011 to 65% in 2015.

Brampton North, Electoral District #35010

Recommended Vote to Keep Your Guns

Vote Conservative.

History at a Glance: 1st and 2nd Place

2004: Liberal over Conservative by 8,203 votes, 20% of votes cast.
2006: Liberal over Conservative by 7,802 votes, 17% of votes cast.
2008: Liberal over Conservative by 773 votes, 1.7% of votes cast.
2011: Conservative over Liberal by 10,397 votes, 20% of votes cast.
2015: Liberal over Conservative by 7,409 votes, 15% of votes cast.

Analysis

This riding typically votes Liberal. Their candidates won four of the past five elections, including Election 2015. Voter turnout rose from 57% in 2011 to 65% in 2015.

Brampton South, Electoral District #35011

Recommended Vote to Keep Your Guns

Vote Conservative.

History at a Glance: 1st and 2nd Place

2015: Liberal over Conservative by 7,752 votes, 17% of votes cast.

Analysis

This electoral district was created prior to the 2015 federal election but voters in this area typically support Liberal candidates.

Brampton West, Electoral District #35012

Recommended Vote to Keep Your Guns

Vote Conservative.

History at a Glance: 1st and 2nd Place

2004: Liberal over Conservative by 2,486 votes, 5.3% of votes cast.
2006: Liberal over Conservative by 7,643 votes, 13% of votes cast.
2008: Liberal over Conservative by 231 votes, 0.4% of votes cast.
2011: Conservative over Liberal by 6,192 votes, 9.8% of votes cast.
2015: Liberal over Conservative by 11,188 votes, 26% of votes cast.

Analysis

This riding typically votes Liberal. Their candidates won four of the past five elections, including Election 2015. Voter turnout rose from 54% in 2011 to 60% in 2015.

Brantford–Brant, Electoral District #35013

Recommended Vote to Keep Your Guns

Vote for Conservative incumbent Phil McColeman.

History at a Glance: 1st and 2nd Place

2004: Liberal over Conservative by 2,663 votes, 5.0% of votes cast.
2006: Liberal over Conservative by 582 votes, 1.0% of votes cast.
2008: Conservative over Liberal by 4,793 votes, 8.8% of votes cast.
2011: Conservative over NDP by 11,694 votes, 20% of votes cast.
2015: Conservative over Liberal by 6,452 votes, 10% of votes cast.

Analysis

This riding tends to vote Conservative. Their candidates won three of the past five elections, including Election 2015. Voter turnout rose from 60% in 2011 to 65% in 2015.

Bruce–Grey–Owen Sound, Electoral District #35014

Recommended Vote to Keep Your Guns

Vote Conservative.

History at a Glance: 1st and 2nd Place

2004: Conservative over Liberal by 4,587 votes, 9.2% of votes cast.
2006: Conservative over Liberal by 10,755 votes, 21% of votes cast.
2008: Conservative over Green by 9,880 votes, 20% of votes cast.
2011: Conservative over NDP by 19,736 votes, 39% of votes cast.
2015: Conservative over Liberal by 4,418 votes, 7.8% of votes cast.

Analysis

This riding typically votes Conservative. Their candidates won the past five elections. Voter turnout rose from 64% in 2011 to 68% in 2015.

Conservative incumbent Larry Miller is retiring.

Burlington, Electoral District #35015

Recommended Vote to Keep Your Guns

Vote Conservative.

History at a Glance: 1st and 2nd Place

2004: Liberal over Conservative by 4,034 votes, 6.6% of votes cast.
2006: Conservative over Liberal by 2,599 votes, 4.0% of votes cast.
2008: Conservative over Liberal by 9,037 votes, 15% of votes cast.
2011: Conservative over Liberal by 18,804 votes, 31% of votes cast.
2015: Liberal over Conservative by 2,449 votes, 3.5% of votes cast.

Analysis

This riding tends to vote Conservative. Their candidates won three of the past five elections. Voter turnout rose from 66% in 2011 to 73% in 2015.

Cambridge, Electoral District #35016

Recommended Vote to Keep Your Guns

Vote Conservative.

History at a Glance: 1st and 2nd Place

2004: Conservative over Liberal by 224 votes, 0.4% of votes cast.
2006: Conservative over Liberal by 5,918 votes, 10% of votes cast.
2008: Conservative over Liberal by 12,918 votes, 25% of votes cast.
2011: Conservative over NDP by 14,156 votes, 26% of votes cast.
2015: Liberal over Conservative by 2,411 votes, 4.5% of votes cast.

Analysis

This riding typically votes Conservative. Their candidates won four of the past five elections. Voter turnout rose from 58% in 2011 to 64% in 2015.

Carleton, Electoral District #35088

Recommended Vote to Keep Your Guns

Vote for Conservative incumbent Pierre Poilievre.

History at a Glance: 1st and 2nd Place

2015: Conservative over Liberal by 1,849 votes, 3.1% of votes cast.

Analysis

Carleton is a new electoral district created by splitting Nepean–Carleton into two separate districts prior to the 2015 federal election. Conservative incumbent Pierre Poilievre has won here since 2004.

Chatham-Kent–Leamington, Electoral District #35017

Recommended Vote to Keep Your Guns

Vote Conservative.

History at a Glance: 1st and 2nd Place

2004: Liberal over Conservative by 407 votes, 0.9% of votes cast.
2006: Conservative over Liberal by 5,616 votes, 12% of votes cast.
2008: Conservative over Liberal by 7,833 votes, 19% of votes cast.
2011: Conservative over NDP by 11,911 votes, 27% of votes cast.
2015: Conservative over Liberal by 2,326 votes, 4.5% of votes cast.

Analysis

This riding typically votes Conservative. Their candidates won four of the past five elections, including Election 2015. Voter turnout rose from 59% in 2011 to 65% in 2015.

Conservative incumbent Dave Van Kesteren retired.

Davenport, Electoral District #35018

Recommended Vote to Keep Your Guns

Vote NDP because they are your best choice to defeat the Liberals.

History at a Glance: 1st and 2nd Place

2004: Liberal over NDP by 5,481 votes, 17% of votes cast.
2006: Liberal over NDP by 7,491 votes, 19% of votes cast.
2008: Liberal over NDP by 5,057 votes, 14% of votes cast.
2011: NDP over Liberal by 10,150 votes, 26% of votes cast.
2015: Liberal over NDP by 1,441 votes, 2.9% of votes cast.

Analysis

This riding typically votes Liberal. Their candidates won four of the past five elections, including Election 2015. Voter turnout rose from 59% in 2011 to 67% in 2015.

Don Valley East, Electoral District #35019

Recommended Vote to Keep Your Guns

Vote Conservative.

History at a Glance: 1st and 2nd Place

2004: Liberal over Conservative by 10,658 votes, 27% of votes cast.
2006: Liberal over Conservative by 10,780 votes, 25% of votes cast.
2008: Liberal over Conservative by 6,487 votes, 17% of votes cast.
2011: Conservative over Liberal by 870 votes, 2.2% of votes cast.
2015: Liberal over Conservative by 11,893 votes, 29% of votes cast.

Analysis

This riding typically votes Liberal. Their candidates won four of the past five elections, including Election 2015. Voter turnout rose from 56% in 2011 to 65% in 2015.

Don Valley North, Electoral District #35020

Recommended Vote to Keep Your Guns

Vote Conservative.

History at a Glance: 1st and 2nd Place

2015: Liberal over Conservative by 6,215 votes, 14% of votes cast.

Analysis

This electoral district was created prior to the 2015 federal election but voters in this area typically support Liberal candidates with the Conservative Party placing second, as they did in Election 2015. The Liberal incumbent will not run for re-election in 2019.

Don Valley West, Electoral District #35021

Recommended Vote to Keep Your Guns

Vote Conservative.

History at a Glance: 1st and 2nd Place

2004: Liberal over Conservative by 16,120 votes, 31% of votes cast.
2006: Liberal over Conservative by 10,801 votes, 20% of votes cast.
2008: Liberal over Conservative by 2,771 votes, 5.5% of votes cast.
2011: Conservative over Liberal by 611 votes, 1.1% of votes cast.
2015: Liberal over Conservative by 8,266 votes, 16% of votes cast.

Analysis

This riding typically votes Liberal. Their candidates won four of the past five elections, including Election 2015. Voter turnout rose from 65% in 2011 to 72% in 2015.

Dufferin–Caledon, Electoral District #35022

Recommended Vote to Keep Your Guns

Vote for Conservative incumbent David Tilson.

History at a Glance: 1st and 2nd Place

2004: Conservative over Liberal by 1,713 votes, 3.8% of votes cast.
2006: Conservative over Liberal by 8,864 votes, 18% of votes cast.
2008: Conservative over Liberal by 14,868 votes, 34% of votes cast.
2011: Conservative over Green by 21,515 votes, 44% of votes cast.
2015: Conservative over Liberal by 4,334 votes, 7.2% of votes cast.

Analysis

This riding typically votes Conservative. Their candidates won the past five elections. Voter turnout rose from 60% in 2011 to 65% in 2015.

Durham, Electoral District #35023

Recommended Vote to Keep Your Guns

Vote for Conservative incumbent Erin O'Toole.

History at a Glance: 1st and 2nd Place

2004: Conservative over Liberal by 1,265 votes, 2.5% of votes cast.
2006: Conservative over Liberal by 9,797 votes, 17% of votes cast.
2008: Conservative over Liberal by 16,384 votes, 31% of votes cast.
2011: Conservative over NDP by 19,460 votes, 33% of votes cast.
2012 By-Election: Conservative over NDP by 8,334 votes, 24% of votes.
2015: Conservative over Liberal by 6,018 votes, 9.4% of votes cast.

Analysis

This riding typically votes Conservative. Their candidates won the past six elections. Voter turnout rose from 63% in 2011 to 68% in 2015.

Eglinton–Lawrence, Electoral District #35024

Recommended Vote to Keep Your Guns

Vote Conservative.

History at a Glance: 1st and 2nd Place

2004: Liberal over Conservative by 16,568 votes, 35% of votes cast.
2006: Liberal over Conservative by 11,147 votes, 23% of votes cast.
2008: Liberal over Conservative by 2,060 votes, 4.7% of votes cast.
2011: Conservative over Liberal by 4,062 votes, 8.4% of votes cast.
2015: Liberal over Conservative by 3,490 votes, 6.3% of votes cast.

Analysis

This riding typically votes Liberal. Their candidates won four of the past five elections, including Election 2015. Voter turnout rose from 66% in 2011 to 71% in 2015.

Elgin–Middlesex–London, Electoral District #35025

Recommended Vote to Keep Your Guns

Vote for Conservative incumbent Karen Louise Vecchio.

History at a Glance: 1st and 2nd Place

2004: Conservative over Liberal by 4,473 votes, 9.6% of votes cast.
2006: Conservative over Liberal by 9,899 votes, 19% of votes cast.
2008: Conservative over Liberal by 11,801 votes, 25% of votes cast.
2011: Conservative over NDP by 16,708 votes, 33% of votes cast.
2015: Conservative over Liberal by 10,381 votes, 18% of votes cast.

Analysis

This riding typically votes Conservative. Their candidates won the past five elections. Voter turnout rose from 62% in 2011 to 68% in 2015.

Essex, Electoral District #35026

Recommended Vote to Keep Your Guns

Vote Conservative.

History at a Glance: 1st and 2nd Place

2004: Conservative over Liberal by 829 votes, 1.6% of votes cast.
2006: Conservative over Liberal by 3,615 votes, 6.3% of votes cast.
2008: Conservative over Liberal by 5,635 votes, 11% of votes cast.
2011: Conservative over NDP by 6,789 votes, 13% of votes cast.
2015: NDP over Conservative by 3,470 votes, 5.7% of votes cast.

Analysis

This riding typically votes Conservative. Their candidates won four of the past five elections. Voter turnout rose from 58% in 2011 to 65% in 2015.

Etobicoke Centre, Electoral District #35027

Recommended Vote to Keep Your Guns

Vote Conservative.

History at a Glance: 1st and 2nd Place

2004: Liberal over Conservative by 15,612 votes, 30% of votes cast.
2006: Liberal over Conservative by 10,807 votes, 19% of votes cast.
2008: Liberal over Conservative by 5,698 votes, 11% of votes cast.
2011: Conservative over Liberal by 26 votes, 0.0% of votes cast.
2015: Liberal over Conservative by 9,542 votes, 15% of votes cast.

Analysis

This riding typically votes Liberal. Their candidates won four of the past five elections, including Election 2015. Voter turnout rose from 64% in 2011 to 70% in 2015.

The one-term Liberal incumbent will not run again in 2019.

Etobicoke North, Electoral District #35029

Recommended Vote to Keep Your Guns

Vote Conservative.

History at a Glance: 1st and 2nd Place

2004: Liberal over Conservative by 13,713 votes, 45% of votes cast.
2006: Liberal over Conservative by 14,146 votes, 39% of votes cast.
2008: Liberal over Conservative by 5,808 votes, 19% of votes cast.
2011: Liberal over Conservative by 3,308 votes, 10% of votes cast.
2015: Liberal over Conservative by 16,578 votes, 39% of votes cast.

Analysis

This riding typically votes Liberal. Their candidates won the past five elections. Voter turnout rose from 51% in 2011 to 60% in 2015.

Etobicoke–Lakeshore, Electoral District #35028

Recommended Vote to Keep Your Guns

Vote Conservative.

History at a Glance: 1st and 2nd Place

2004: Liberal over Conservative by 9,750 votes, 20% of votes cast.
2006: Liberal over Conservative by 4,724 votes, 8.5% of votes cast.
2008: Liberal over Conservative by 5,743 votes, 11% of votes cast.
2011: Conservative over Liberal by 2,869 votes, 5.3% of votes cast.
2015: Liberal over Conservative by 13,706 votes, 21% of votes cast

Analysis

This riding typically votes Liberal. Their candidates won four of the past five elections, including Election 2015. Voter turnout rose from 63% in 2011 to 69% in 2015.

Flamborough–Glanbrook, Electoral District #35030

Recommended Vote to Keep Your Guns

Vote for Conservative incumbent David Sweet.

History at a Glance: 1st and 2nd Place

2015: Conservative over Liberal by 2,409 votes, 4.3% of votes cast.

Analysis

This electoral district was created prior to the 2015 federal election.

Glengarry–Prescott–Russell, Electoral District #35031

Recommended Vote to Keep Your Guns

Vote Conservative.

History at a Glance: 1st and 2nd Place

2004: Liberal over Conservative by 5,192 votes, 10% of votes cast.
2006: Conservative over Liberal by 203 votes, 0.4% of votes cast.
2008: Conservative over Liberal by 5,662 votes, 10% of votes cast.
2011: Conservative over Liberal by 10,469 votes, 18% of votes cast.
2015: Liberal over Conservative by 10,822 votes, 17% of votes cast.

Analysis

This riding tends to vote Conservative. Their candidates won three of the past five elections. Liberals won in Election 2015 by 10,822 votes. Voter turnout rose from 68% in 2011 to 75% in 2015.

Guelph, Electoral District #35032

Recommended Vote to Keep Your Guns

Vote Conservative.

History at a Glance: 1st and 2nd Place

2004: Liberal over Conservative by 9,721 votes, 18% of votes cast.
2006: Liberal over Conservative by 5,320 votes, 8.6% of votes cast.
2008: Liberal over Conservative by 1,788 votes, 2.5% of votes cast.
2011: Liberal over Conservative by 6,236 votes, 7.4% of votes cast.
2015: Liberal over Conservative by 15,896 votes, 23% of votes cast.

Analysis

This riding typically votes Liberal. Their candidates won the past five elections. Voter turnout dropped from 93% in 2011 to 71% in 2015.

Haldimand–Norfolk, Electoral District #35033

Recommended Vote to Keep Your Guns

Vote for Conservative incumbent Diane Finley.

History at a Glance: 1st and 2nd Place

2004: Conservative over Liberal by 1,645 votes, 3.3% of votes cast.
2006: Conservative over Liberal by 7,522 votes, 14% of votes cast.
2008: Conservative over Liberal by 4,080 votes, 8.5% of votes cast.
2011: Conservative over Liberal by 13,106 votes, 26% of votes cast.
2015: Conservative over Liberal by 4,227 votes, 7.5% of votes cast.

Analysis

This riding typically votes Conservative. Their candidates won the past five elections. Voter turnout rose from 62% in 2011 to 67% in 2015.

Haliburton–Kawartha Lakes–Brock, Electoral District #35034

Recommended Vote to Keep Your Guns

Vote for Conservative incumbent Jamie Schmale.

History at a Glance: 1st and 2nd Place

2004: Conservative over Liberal by 5,127 votes, 9.2% of votes cast.
2006: Conservative over Liberal by 11,574 votes, 19% of votes cast.
2008: Conservative over Liberal by 19,190 votes, 35% of votes cast.
2011: Conservative over NDP by 21,855 votes, 37% of votes cast.
2015: Conservative over Liberal by 8,084 votes, 13% of votes cast.

Analysis

This riding typically votes Conservative. Their candidates won the past five elections. Voter turnout rose from 63% in 2011 to 67% in 2015.

Hamilton Centre, Electoral District #35035

Recommended Vote to Keep Your Guns

Vote NDP because they are our best choice to defeat the Liberals.

History at a Glance: 1st and 2nd Place

2004: NDP over Liberal by 5,373 votes, 12% of votes cast.
2006: NDP over Liberal by 13,279 votes, 28% of votes cast.
2008: NDP over Conservative by 10,959 votes, 27% of votes cast.
2011: NDP over Conservative by 12,829 votes, 31% of votes cast.
2015: NDP over Liberal by 5,001 votes, 12% of votes cast.

Analysis

This riding typically votes NDP. Their candidates won the past five elections. Voter turnout rose from 53% in 2011 to 59% in 2015. The NDP incumbent who represented this electoral district since 2004 will not run again in 2019.

Hamilton East–Stoney Creek, Electoral District #35036

Recommended Vote to Keep Your Guns

Vote NDP because they are your best choice to defeat the Liberals.

History at a Glance: 1st and 2nd Place

2004: Liberal over NDP by 927 votes, 1.9% of votes cast.
2006: NDP over Liberal by 466 votes, 0.9% of votes cast.
2008: NDP over Liberal by 6,464 votes, 13% of votes cast.
2011: NDP over Conservative by 4,364 votes, 10% of votes cast.
2015: Liberal over NDP by 3,157 votes, 6.3% of votes cast.

Analysis

This riding tends to vote NDP. Their candidates won three of the past five elections and the primary battle is between Liberal and NDP. Voter turnout rose from 50% in 2011 to 62% in 2015.

Hamilton Mountain, Electoral District #35037

Recommended Vote to Keep Your Guns

Vote for NDP incumbent Scott Duvall.

History at a Glance: 1st and 2nd Place

2004: Liberal over NDP by 996 votes, 1.9% of votes cast.
2006: NDP over Liberal by 3,266 votes, 5.6% of votes cast.
2008: NDP over Conservative by 6,786 votes, 13% of votes cast.
2011: NDP over Conservative by 7,659 votes, 14% of votes cast.
2015: NDP over Liberal by 1,213 votes, 2.4% of votes cast.

Analysis

This riding typically votes NDP. Their candidates won four of the past five elections, including Election 2015. Voter turnout rose from 61% in 2011 to 65% in 2015.

Hamilton West–Ancaster–Dundas, Electoral District #35038

Recommended Vote to Keep Your Guns

Vote Conservative.

History at a Glance: 1st and 2nd Place

2004: Liberal over Conservative by 2,800 votes, 5.1% of votes cast.
2006: Conservative over Liberal by 2,874 votes, 4.6% of votes cast.
2008: Conservative over Liberal by 10,975 votes, 19% of votes cast.
2011: Conservative over Liberal by 15,646 votes, 27% of votes cast.
2015: Liberal over Conservative by 9,873 votes, 16% of votes cast.

Analysis

This riding tends to vote Conservative. Their candidates won three of the past five elections. Liberals won in Election 2015 by 9,873 votes. Voter turnout rose from 68% in 2011 to 72% in 2015.

Hastings–Lennox and Addington, Electoral District #35039

Recommended Vote to Keep Your Guns

Vote Conservative.

History at a Glance: 1st and 2nd Place

2015: Liberal over Conservative by 225 votes, 0.5% of votes cast.

Analysis

This electoral district was created prior to the 2015 federal election but voters in this area typically support Conservative candidates.

Humber River–Black Creek, Electoral District #35121

Recommended Vote to Keep Your Guns

Vote NDP because they are your best choice to defeat the Liberals.

History at a Glance: 1st and 2nd Place

2004: Liberal over NDP by 13,675 votes, 49% of votes cast.
2006: Liberal over Conservative by 15,174 votes, 45% of votes cast.
2008: Liberal over NDP by 11,634 votes, 41% of votes cast.
2011: Liberal over NDP by 5,309 votes, 19% of votes cast.
2015: Liberal over Conservative by 16,767 votes, 47% of votes cast.

Analysis

This riding typically votes Liberal. Their candidates won the past five elections. Voter turnout rose from 48% in 2011 to 57% in 2015.

Huron–Bruce, Electoral District #35040

Recommended Vote to Keep Your Guns

Vote for Conservative incumbent Ben Lobb.

History at a Glance: 1st and 2nd Place

2004: Liberal over Conservative by 9,608 votes, 19% of votes cast.
2006: Liberal over Conservative by 971 votes, 1.8% of votes cast.
2008: Conservative over Liberal by 5,846 votes, 12% of votes cast.
2011: Conservative over NDP by 15,762 votes, 30% of votes cast.
2015: Conservative over Liberal by 3,045 votes, 5.2% of votes cast.

Analysis

This riding tends to vote Conservative. Their candidates won three of the past five elections, including Election 2015. Voter turnout rose from 68% in 2011 to 72% in 2015.

Kanata–Carleton, Electoral District #35041

Recommended Vote to Keep Your Guns

Vote Conservative.

History at a Glance: 1st and 2nd Place

2004: Conservative over Liberal by 10,479 votes, 16% of votes cast.
2006: Conservative over Liberal by 22,644 votes, 33% of votes cast.
2008: Conservative over Liberal by 24,179 votes, 35% of votes cast.
2011: Conservative over Liberal by 25,330 votes, 33% of votes cast.
2015: Liberal over Conservative by 7,648 votes, 12% of votes cast.

Analysis

This riding typically votes Conservative. Their candidates won four of the past five elections. Voter turnout rose from 71% in 2011 to 79% in 2015.

Kenora, Electoral District #35042

Recommended Vote to Keep Your Guns

Vote Conservative.

History at a Glance: 1st and 2nd Place

2004: Liberal over NDP by 982 votes, 4.2% of votes cast.
2006: Liberal over Conservative by 1,503 votes, 5.5% of votes cast.
2008: Conservative over Liberal by 2,051 votes, 8.8% of votes cast.
2011: Conservative over NDP by 4,712 votes, 19% of votes cast.
2015: Liberal over NDP by 441 votes, 1.4% of votes cast.

Analysis

This riding tends to vote Liberal although the Conservatives won here in 2008 and 2011 before losing a tight race in 2015. Liberal candidates won three of the past five elections, including Election 2015. Voter turnout rose from 58% in 2011 to 70% in 2015.

Kingston and the Islands, Electoral District #35044

Recommended Vote to Keep Your Guns

Vote Conservative.

History at a Glance: 1st and 2nd Place

2004: Liberal over Conservative by 15,962 votes, 29% of votes cast.
2006: Liberal over Conservative by 12,318 votes, 20% of votes cast.
2008: Liberal over Conservative by 3,839 votes, 6.6% of votes cast.
2011: Liberal over Conservative by 2,653 votes, 4.4% of votes cast.
2015: Liberal over Conservative by 21,493 votes, 33% of votes cast.

Analysis

This riding typically votes Liberal. Their candidates won the past five elections. Voter turnout rose from 63% in 2011 to 70% in 2015.

King–Vaughan, Electoral District #35043

Recommended Vote to Keep Your Guns

Vote Conservative.

History at a Glance: 1st and 2nd Place

2015: Liberal over Conservative by 1,738 votes, 3.2% of votes cast.

Analysis

This electoral district was created prior to the 2015 federal election.

Kitchener Centre, Electoral District #35045

Recommended Vote to Keep Your Guns

Vote Conservative.

History at a Glance: 1st and 2nd Place

2004: Liberal over Conservative by 8,852 votes, 20% of votes cast.
2006: Liberal over Conservative by 5,583 votes, 11% of votes cast.
2008: Conservative over Liberal by 339 votes, 0.8% of votes cast.
2011: Conservative over Liberal by 5,527 votes, 11% of votes cast.
2015: Liberal over Conservative by 9,632 votes, 18% of votes cast.

Analysis

This riding tends to vote Liberal. Their candidates won three of the past five elections, including Election 2015. Voter turnout rose from 62% in 2011 to 67% in 2015.

Kitchener South–Hespeler, Electoral District #35047

Recommended Vote to Keep Your Guns

Vote Conservative.

History at a Glance: 1st and 2nd Place

2015: Liberal over Conservative by 2,671 votes, 5.6% of votes cast.

Analysis

This electoral district was created prior to the 2015 federal election.

Kitchener–Conestoga, Electoral District #35046

Recommended Vote to Keep Your Guns

Vote for Conservative incumbent Harold Albrecht.

History at a Glance: 1st and 2nd Place

2004: Liberal over Conservative by 2,916 votes, 6.9% of votes cast.
2006: Conservative over Liberal by 1,369 votes, 2.7% of votes cast.
2008: Conservative over Liberal by 11,649 votes, 24% of votes cast.
2011: Conservative over NDP by 17,237 votes, 32% of votes cast.
2015: Conservative over Liberal by 251 votes, 0.5% of votes cast.

Analysis

This riding typically votes Conservative. Their candidates won four of the past five elections, including Election 2015. Voter turnout rose from 60% in 2011 to 69% in 2015.

Lambton–Kent–Middlesex, Electoral District #35048

Recommended Vote to Keep Your Guns

Vote Conservative.

History at a Glance: 1st and 2nd Place

2004: Liberal over Conservative by 164 votes, 0.3% of votes cast.
2006: Conservative over Liberal by 8,335 votes, 15% of votes cast.
2008: Conservative over Liberal by 12,704 votes, 27% of votes cast.
2011: Conservative over NDP by 17,247 votes, 34% of votes cast.
2015: Conservative over Liberal by 11,708 votes, 21% of votes cast.

Analysis

This riding typically votes Conservative. Their candidates won four of the past five elections, including Election 2015. Voter turnout rose from 64% in 2011 to 69% in 2015.

Conservative incumbent Bev Shipley will not run again in 2019.

Lanark–Frontenac–Kingston, Electoral District #35049

Recommended Vote to Keep Your Guns

Vote for Conservative incumbent Scott Reid.

History at a Glance: 1st and 2nd Place

2004: Conservative over Liberal by 10,059 votes, 18% of votes cast.
2006: Conservative over Liberal by 15,658 votes, 26% of votes cast.
2008: Conservative over Liberal by 18,463 votes, 34% of votes cast.
2011: Conservative over NDP by 21,580 votes, 37% of votes cast.
2015: Conservative over Liberal by 8,074 votes, 14% of votes cast.

Analysis

This riding typically votes Conservative. Their candidates won the past five elections. Voter turnout rose from 64% in 2011 to 72% in 2015.

Leeds–Grenville–Thousand Islands and Rideau Lakes, Electoral District #35050

Recommended Vote to Keep Your Guns

Vote for Conservative incumbent Michael Barrett.

History at a Glance: 1st and 2nd Place

2004: Conservative over Liberal by 9,035 votes, 18% of votes cast.
2006: Conservative over Liberal by 15,786 votes, 30% of votes cast.
2008: Conservative over Liberal by 19,398 votes, 41% of votes cast.
2011: Conservative over NDP by 20,958 votes, 42% of votes cast.
2015: Conservative over Liberal by 3,707 votes, 6.6% of votes cast.
2018 By-Election: Conservative over Liberal by 6,405 votes, 22% of votes cast.

Analysis

This riding typically votes Conservative and their candidates won the past six elections. Voter turnout rose from 64% in 2011 to 70% in 2015.

London North Centre, Electoral District #35052

Recommended Vote to Keep Your Guns

Vote Conservative.

History at a Glance: 1st and 2nd Place

2004: Liberal over Conservative by 7,795 votes, 16% of votes cast.
2006: Liberal over Conservative by 6,141 votes, 10% of votes cast.
2008: Liberal over Conservative by 3,306 votes, 6.2% of votes cast.
2011: Conservative over Liberal by 1,665 votes, 3.2% of votes cast.
2015: Liberal over Conservative by 12,437 votes, 19% of votes cast.

Analysis

This riding typically votes Liberal. Their candidates won four of the past five elections, including Election 2015. Voter turnout rose from 60% in 2011 to 69% in 2015.

London West, Electoral District #35053

Recommended Vote to Keep Your Guns

Vote Conservative.

History at a Glance: 1st and 2nd Place

2004: Liberal over Conservative by 7,726 votes, 14% of votes cast.
2006: Liberal over Conservative by 1,329 votes, 2.2% of votes cast.
2008: Conservative over Liberal by 2,121 votes, 3.7% of votes cast.
2011: Conservative over Liberal by 11,023 votes, 18% of votes cast.
2015: Liberal over Conservative by 7,131 votes, 10% of votes cast.

Analysis

Liberals won three of the past five elections, including Election 2015. Voter turnout rose from 66% in 2011 to 73% in 2015.

London–Fanshawe, Electoral District #35051

Recommended Vote to Keep Your Guns

Vote NDP because they are your best choice to defeat the Liberals.

History at a Glance: 1st and 2nd Place

2004: Liberal over NDP by 3,153 votes, 7.7% of votes cast.
2006: NDP over Liberal by 868 votes, 1.9% of votes cast.
2008: NDP over Conservative by 5,013 votes, 12% of votes cast.
2011: NDP over Conservative by 7,395 votes, 17% of votes cast.
2015: NDP over Liberal by 3,470 votes, 6.3% of votes cast.

Analysis

This riding typically votes NDP. Their candidates won four of the past five elections, including Election 2015. Voter turnout rose from 57% in 2011 to 63% in 2015.

The NDP incumbent who represented this electoral district since 2006 will not run again in 2019.

Markham–Stouffville, Electoral District #35054

Recommended Vote to Keep Your Guns

Vote Conservative.

History at a Glance: 1st and 2nd Place

2004: Liberal over Conservative by 11,252 votes, 18% of votes cast.
2006: Liberal over Conservative by 6,400 votes, 8.6% of votes cast.
2008: Conservative over Liberal by 545 votes, 0.7% of votes cast.
2011: Conservative over Liberal by 20,680 votes, 23% of votes cast.
2015: Liberal over Conservative by 3,851 votes, 6.4% of votes cast.

Analysis

Liberals won three of the past five elections, including Election 2015. Voter turnout rose from 59% in 2011 to 68% in 2015.

Markham–Thornhill, Electoral District #35055

Recommended Vote to Keep Your Guns

Vote Conservative.

History at a Glance: 1st and 2nd Place

2015: Liberal over Conservative by 10,029 votes, 23% of votes cast.
2017 By-Election: Liberal over Conservative by 2,380 votes, 12% of votes cast.

Analysis

Liberals won both elections in this riding since it was created.

Markham–Unionville, Electoral District #35056

Recommended Vote to Keep Your Guns

Vote for Conservative incumbent Bob Saroya.

History at a Glance: 1st and 2nd Place

2004: Liberal over Conservative by 20,117 votes, 44% of votes cast.
2006: Liberal over Conservative by 18,616 votes, 35% of votes cast.
2008: Liberal over Conservative by 11,441 votes, 25% of votes cast.
2011: Liberal over Conservative by 1,695 votes, 3.4% of votes cast.
2015: Conservative over Liberal by 3,009 votes, 6.0% of votes cast.

Analysis

Liberals won four of the past five elections. Voter turnout rose from 54% in 2011 to 60% in 2015.

Milton, Electoral District #35057

Recommended Vote to Keep Your Guns

Vote for Conservative incumbent Lisa Raitt.

History at a Glance: 1st and 2nd Place

2015: Conservative over Liberal by 2,438 votes, 4.9% of votes cast.

Analysis

This electoral district was created prior to the 2015 federal election and voters in this area typically support Conservative candidates. Long-time Conservative MP Lisa Raitt won a relatively tight race here in 2015.

Mississauga Centre, Electoral District #35058

Recommended Vote to Keep Your Guns

Vote Conservative.

History at a Glance: 1st and 2nd Place

2015: Liberal over Conservative by 10,941 votes, 21% of votes cast.

Analysis

This electoral district was created prior to the 2015 federal election.

Mississauga East–Cooksville, Electoral District #35059

Recommended Vote to Keep Your Guns

Vote Conservative.

History at a Glance: 1st and 2nd Place

2004: Liberal over Conservative by 12,136 votes, 31% of votes cast.
2006: Liberal over Conservative by 9,204 votes, 20% of votes cast.
2008: Liberal over Conservative by 7,180 votes, 18% of votes cast.
2011: Conservative over Liberal by 676 votes, 1.4% of votes cast.
2015: Liberal over Conservative by 9,801 votes, 19% of votes cast.

Analysis

This riding typically votes Liberal. Their candidates won four of the past five elections, including Election 2015. Voter turnout rose from 55% in 2011 to 63% in 2015.

Mississauga–Erin Mills, Electoral District #35060

Recommended Vote to Keep Your Guns

Vote Conservative.

History at a Glance: 1st and 2nd Place

2004: Liberal over Conservative by 11,646 votes, 22% of votes cast.
2006: Liberal over Conservative by 3,328 votes, 5.6% of votes cast.
2008: Conservative over Liberal by 397 votes, 0.7% of votes cast.
2011: Conservative over Liberal by 8,252 votes, 13% of votes cast.
2015: Liberal over Conservative by 5,804 votes, 10% of votes cast.

Analysis

This riding tends to vote Liberal. Their candidates won three of the past five elections, including Election 2015. Voter turnout rose from 60% in 2011 to 67% in 2015.

Mississauga–Lakeshore, Electoral District #35061

Recommended Vote to Keep Your Guns

Vote Conservative.

History at a Glance: 1st and 2nd Place

2004: Liberal over Conservative by 8,601 votes, 18% of votes cast.
2006: Liberal over Conservative by 2,130 votes, 4.1% of votes cast.
2008: Liberal over Conservative by 2,152 votes, 4.6% of votes cast.
2011: Conservative over Liberal by 4,598 votes, 9.3% of votes cast.
2015: Liberal over Conservative by 3,844 votes, 6.5% of votes cast.

Analysis

This riding typically votes Liberal. Their candidates won four of the past five elections, including Election 2015. Voter turnout rose from 63% in 2011 to 68% in 2015.

Mississauga–Malton, Electoral District #35062

Recommended Vote to Keep Your Guns

Vote Conservative.

History at a Glance: 1st and 2nd Place

2004: Liberal over Conservative by 14,320 votes, 33% of votes cast.
2006: Liberal over Conservative by 11,765 votes, 23% of votes cast.
2008: Liberal over Conservative by 6,556 votes, 15% of votes cast.
2011: Conservative over Liberal by 5,053 votes, 9.6% of votes cast.
2015: Liberal over Conservative by 14,464 votes, 33% of votes cast.

Analysis

This riding typically votes Liberal. Their candidates won four of the past five elections, including Election 2015. Voter turnout rose from 56% in 2011 to 59% in 2015.

Mississauga–Streetsville, Electoral District #35063

Recommended Vote to Keep Your Guns

Vote Conservative.

History at a Glance: 1st and 2nd Place

2004: Liberal over Conservative by 8,481 votes, 19% of votes cast.
2006: Liberal over Conservative by 5,792 votes, 11% of votes cast.
2008: Liberal over Conservative by 4,725 votes, 10.0% of votes cast.
2011: Conservative over Liberal by 3,453 votes, 6.9% of votes cast.
2015: Liberal over Conservative by 4,171 votes, 7.4% of votes cast.

Analysis

Liberals won four of the past five elections, including Election 2015.
Voter turnout rose from 58% in 2011 to 67% in 2015.

Nepean, Electoral District #35064

Recommended Vote to Keep Your Guns

Vote Conservative.

History at a Glance: 1st and 2nd Place

2004: Conservative over Liberal by 3,736 votes, 5.6% of votes cast.
2006: Conservative over Liberal by 19,401 votes, 27% of votes cast.
2008: Conservative over Liberal by 23,178 votes, 32% of votes cast.
2011: Conservative over Liberal by 23,331 votes, 29% of votes cast.
2015: Liberal over Conservative by 10,575 votes, 12% of votes cast.

Analysis

Election 2015 was the first win for Liberals in the past five elections,
assisted by a rise in voter turnout, which increased from 71% in 2011
to 78% in 2015.

Newmarket–Aurora, Electoral District #35065

Recommended Vote to Keep Your Guns

Vote Conservative.

History at a Glance: 1st and 2nd Place

2004: Conservative over Liberal by 689 votes, 1.3% of votes cast.
2006: Liberal over Conservative by 4,800 votes, 8.2% of votes cast.
2008: Conservative over Liberal by 6,623 votes, 12% of votes cast.
2011: Conservative over Liberal by 17,692 votes, 30% of votes cast.
2015: Liberal over Conservative by 1,451 votes, 2.6% of votes cast.

Analysis

Liberals won three of the past five elections, including Election 2015. Voter turnout rose from 63% in 2011 to 68% in 2015.35035

Niagara Centre, Electoral District #35066

Recommended Vote to Keep Your Guns

Vote NDP because they are your best choice to defeat the Liberals.

History at a Glance: 1st and 2nd Place

2004: Liberal over NDP by 5,019 votes, 10% of votes cast.
2006: Liberal over NDP by 2,775 votes, 4.9% of votes cast.
2008: NDP over Conservative by 300 votes, 0.6% of votes cast.
2011: NDP over Conservative by 1,022 votes, 2.0% of votes cast.
2015: Liberal over NDP by 2,295 votes, 4.2% of votes cast.

Analysis

Liberals won three of the past five elections, including Election 2015. Voter turnout rose from 61% in 2011 to 65% in 2015.

Niagara Falls, Electoral District #35067

Recommended Vote to Keep Your Guns

Vote Conservative.

History at a Glance: 1st and 2nd Place

2004: Conservative over Liberal by 1,137 votes, 2.2% of votes cast
2006: Conservative over Liberal by 3,393 votes, 5.8% of votes cast.
2008: Conservative over Liberal by 10,149 votes, 20% of votes cast.
2011: Conservative over NDP by 16,067 votes, 30% of votes cast.
2015: Conservative over Liberal by 4,917 votes, 7.6% of votes cast.

Analysis:

Conservative incumbent Rob Nicholson won the past five elections and is retiring. Voter turnout rose from 56% in 2011 to 63% in 2015.

Niagara West, Electoral District #35068

Recommended Vote to Keep Your Guns

Vote for Conservative incumbent Dean Allison.

History at a Glance: 1st and 2nd Place

2004: Conservative over Liberal by 664 votes, 1.3% of votes cast.
2006: Conservative over Liberal by 9,639 votes, 17% of votes cast.
2008: Conservative over Liberal by 15,134 votes, 28% of votes cast.
2011: Conservative over NDP by 20,967 votes, 36% of votes cast.
2015: Conservative over Liberal by 8,151 votes, 16% of votes cast.

Analysis

This riding typically votes Conservative and Dean Allison won the past five elections. Voter turnout rose from 66% in 2011 to 73% in 2015.

Nickel Belt, Electoral District #35069

Recommended Vote to Keep Your Guns

Vote NDP because they are your best choice to defeat the Liberals.

History at a Glance: 1st and 2nd Place

2004: Liberal over NDP by 3,208 votes, 7.9% of votes cast.
2006: Liberal over NDP by 2,107 votes, 4.6% of votes cast.
2008: NDP over Liberal by 8,273 votes, 20% of votes cast.
2011: NDP over Conservative by 12,063 votes, 27% of votes cast.
2015: Liberal over NDP by 2,654 votes, 5.4% of votes cast.

Analysis

This riding tends to vote Liberal. Their candidates won three of the past five elections, including Election 2015. Voter turnout rose from 62% in 2011 to 67% in 2015.

Nipissing–Timiskaming, Electoral District #35070

Recommended Vote to Keep Your Guns

Vote Conservative.

History at a Glance: 1st and 2nd Place

2004: Liberal over Conservative by 2,253 votes, 5.2% of votes cast.
2006: Liberal over Conservative by 4,882 votes, 10% of votes cast.
2008: Liberal over Conservative by 5,078 votes, 12% of votes cast.
2011: Conservative over Liberal by 18 votes, 0.04% of votes cast.
2015: Liberal over Conservative by 11,032 votes, 23% of votes cast.

Analysis

This riding typically votes Liberal. Their candidates won four of the past five elections, including Election 2015. Voter turnout rose from 60% in 2011 to 68% in 2015.

Northumberland–Peterborough South, Electoral District #35071

Recommended Vote to Keep Your Guns

Vote Conservative.

History at a Glance: 1st and 2nd Place

2004: Liberal over Conservative by 313 votes, 0.5% of votes cast.
2006: Conservative over Liberal by 3,267 votes, 5.2% of votes cast.
2008: Conservative over Liberal by 11,406 votes, 20% of votes cast.
2011: Conservative over Liberal by 20,031 votes, 33% of votes cast.
2015: Liberal over Conservative by 1,878 votes, 3.0% of votes cast.

Analysis

This riding tends to vote Conservative. Their candidates won three of the past five elections. Voter turnout rose from 63% in 2011 to 71% in 2015.

Oakville, Electoral District #35072

Recommended Vote to Keep Your Guns

Vote Conservative.

History at a Glance: 1st and 2nd Place

2004: Liberal over Conservative by 9,205 votes, 17% of votes cast.
2006: Liberal over Conservative by 744 votes, 1.2% of votes cast.
2008: Conservative over Liberal by 5,483 votes, 9.9% of votes cast.
2011: Conservative over Liberal by 12,178 votes, 21% of votes cast.
2015: Liberal over Conservative by 4,459 votes, 6.9% of votes cast.

Analysis

This riding tends to vote Liberal. Their candidates won three of the past five elections, including Election 2015, when voter turnout rose from 68% in 2011.

The Liberal incumbent will not run again in 2019, leaving the door open for Conservatives to retake this electoral district in 2019.

Oakville North–Burlington, Electoral District #35073

Recommended Vote to Keep Your Guns

Vote Conservative.

History at a Glance: 1st and 2nd Place

2004: Liberal over Conservative by 5,658 votes, 10.0% of votes cast.
2006: Conservative over Liberal by 1,897 votes, 2.7% of votes cast.
2008: Conservative over Liberal by 7,850 votes, 11% of votes cast.
2011: Conservative over Liberal by 23,311 votes, 29% of votes cast.
2015: Liberal over Conservative by 2,073 votes, 3.4% of votes cast.

Analysis

This riding tends to vote Conservative. The Liberal incumbent works against gun owners and is a candidate for defeat in 2019.

Voter turnout rose from 61% in 2011 to 71% in 2015.

Orléans, Electoral District #35076

Recommended Vote to Keep Your Guns

Vote Conservative.

History at a Glance: 1st and 2nd Place

2004: Liberal over Conservative by 2,728 votes, 4.7% of votes cast.
2006: Conservative over Liberal by 1,231 votes, 2.0% of votes cast.
2008: Conservative over Liberal by 3,695 votes, 6.1% of votes cast.
2011: Conservative over Liberal by 3,935 votes, 6.1% of votes cast.
2015: Liberal over Conservative by 22,721 votes, 29% of votes cast.

Analysis

Conservatives won three of the past five elections. Voter turnout rose from 71% in 2011 to 80% in 2015.

The first-term Liberal incumbent will not run again in 2019.

Oshawa, Electoral District #35074

Recommended Vote to Keep Your Guns

Vote for Conservative incumbent Colin Carrie.

History at a Glance: 1st and 2nd Place

2004: Conservative over NDP by 463 votes, 1.0% of votes cast.
2006: Conservative over NDP by 2,752 votes, 5.1% of votes cast.
2008: Conservative over NDP by 3,201 votes, 6.6% of votes cast.
2011: Conservative over NDP by 6,822 votes, 13% of votes cast.
2015: Conservative over NDP by 3,823 votes, 6.3% of votes cast.

Analysis

This riding typically votes Conservative. Their candidates won the past five elections. Voter turnout rose from 57% in 2011 to 63% in 2015.

Ottawa Centre, Electoral District #35075

Recommended Vote to Keep Your Guns

Vote NDP because they are your best choice to defeat the Liberals.

History at a Glance: 1st and 2nd Place

2004: NDP over Liberal by 6,256 votes, 8.4% of votes cast.
2006: NDP over Liberal by 5,141 votes, 7.7% of votes cast.
2008: NDP over Liberal by 8,766 votes, 14% of votes cast.
2011: NDP over Conservative by 19,742 votes, 30% of votes cast.
2015: Liberal over NDP by 3,113 votes, 4.1% of votes cast.

Analysis

Election 2015 was the first win for the Liberals after at least four NDP victories. Voter turnout rose from 72% in 2011 to 80% in 2015.

Ottawa South, Electoral District #35077

Recommended Vote to Keep Your Guns

Vote Conservative.

History at a Glance: 1st and 2nd Place

2004: Liberal over Conservative by 5,334 votes, 8.9% of votes cast.
2006: Liberal over Conservative by 4,130 votes, 6.7% of votes cast.
2008: Liberal over Conservative by 9,618 votes, 17% of votes cast.
2011: Liberal over Conservative by 6,329 votes, 11% of votes cast.
2015: Liberal over Conservative by 23,120 votes, 36% of votes cast.

Analysis

This riding typically votes Liberal. Voter turnout rose from 67% in 2011 to 73% in 2015.

Ottawa West–Nepean, Electoral District #35079

Recommended Vote to Keep Your Guns

Vote Conservative.

History at a Glance: 1st and 2nd Place

2004: Liberal over Conservative by 1,380 votes, 2.4% of votes cast.
2006: Conservative over Liberal by 5,357 votes, 9.0% of votes cast.
2008: Conservative over Liberal by 4,948 votes, 8.9% of votes cast.
2011: Conservative over Liberal by 7,436 votes, 13% of votes cast.
2015: Liberal over Conservative by 16,306 votes, 26% of votes cast.

Analysis

This riding tends to vote Conservative. Their candidates won three of the past five elections.

Voter turnout rose from 68% in 2011 to 74% in 2015.

Ottawa–Vanier, Electoral District #35078

Recommended Vote to Keep Your Guns

Vote NDP because they are your best choice to defeat the Liberals.

History at a Glance: 1st and 2nd Place

2004: Liberal over Conservative by 13,183 votes, 25% of votes cast.
2006: Liberal over Conservative by 7,597 votes, 14% of votes cast.
2008: Liberal over Conservative by 9,810 votes, 19% of votes cast.
2011: Liberal over NDP by 4,618 votes, 8.8% of votes cast.
2015: Liberal over NDP by 24,280 votes, 38% of votes cast.
2017 By-Election: Liberal over NDP by 6,638 votes, 22% of votes cast.

Analysis

This riding typically votes Liberal. Voter turnout rose from 66% in 2011 to 73% in 2015.

Oxford, Electoral District #35080

Recommended Vote to Keep Your Guns

Vote for Conservative incumbent Dave MacKenzie.

History at a Glance: 1st and 2nd Place

2004: Conservative over Liberal by 6,595 votes, 14% of votes cast.
2006: Conservative over Liberal by 9,179 votes, 18% of votes cast.
2008: Conservative over Liberal by 14,744 votes, 33% of votes cast.
2011: Conservative over NDP by 15,809 votes, 33% of votes cast.
2015: Conservative over Liberal by 7,667 votes, 13% of votes cast.

Analysis

This riding typically votes Conservative and Dave MacKenzie won the past five elections. Voter turnout rose from 62% in 2011 to 68% in 2015.

Parkdale–High Park, Electoral District #35081

Recommended Vote to Keep Your Guns

Vote NDP because they are your best choice to defeat the Liberals.

History at a Glance: 1st and 2nd Place

2004: Liberal over NDP by 3,526 votes, 7.5% of votes cast.
2006: NDP over Liberal by 2,301 votes, 4.5% of votes cast.
2008: Liberal over NDP by 3,373 votes, 7.0% of votes cast.
2011: NDP over Liberal by 7,289 votes, 14% of votes cast.
2015: Liberal over NDP by 1,057 votes, 1.3% of votes cast.

Analysis

Liberals won three of the past five elections, including Election 2015. Voter turnout rose from 68% in 2011 to 73% in 2015.

Parry Sound–Muskoka, Electoral District #35082

Recommended Vote to Keep Your Guns

Vote Conservative.

History at a Glance: 1st and 2nd Place

2004: Liberal over Conservative by 3,301 votes.
2006: Conservative over Liberal by 28 votes.
2008: Conservative over Liberal by 10,960 votes.
2011: Conservative over NDP by 14,647 votes.
2015: Conservative over Liberal by 2,269 votes.

Analysis

This riding typically votes Conservative. Their candidates won four of the past five elections, including Election 2015. Voter turnout rose from 65% in 2011 to 67% in 2015.

Perth–Wellington, Electoral District #35083

Recommended Vote to Keep Your Guns

Vote for Conservative incumbent John Nater.

History at a Glance: 1st and 2nd Place

2004: Conservative over Liberal by 3,847 votes, 8.6% of votes cast.
2006: Conservative over Liberal by 9,703 votes, 20% of votes cast.
2008: Conservative over Liberal by 10,540 votes, 24% of votes cast.
2011: Conservative over NDP by 15,420 votes, 33% of votes cast.
2015: Conservative over Liberal by 2,775 votes, 5.4% of votes cast.

Analysis

This riding typically votes Conservative. Their candidates won the past five elections. Voter turnout rose from 63% in 2011 to 68% in 2015.

Peterborough–Kawartha, Electoral District #35084

Recommended Vote to Keep Your Guns

Vote Conservative.

History at a Glance: 1st and 2nd Place

2004: Liberal over Conservative by 6,706 votes, 12% of votes cast.
2006: Conservative over Liberal by 2,242 votes, 3.5% of votes cast.
2008: Conservative over Liberal by 9,213 votes, 16% of votes cast.
2011: Conservative over NDP by 14,670 votes, 25% of votes cast.
2015: Liberal over Conservative by 5,824 votes, 8.8% of votes cast.

Analysis

This electoral district is a priority for Conservatives to win back in Election 2019.

Voter turnout rose from 64.53% in 2011 to 71.40% in 2015.

Pickering–Uxbridge, Electoral District #35085

Recommended Vote to Keep Your Guns

Vote Conservative.

History at a Glance: 1st and 2nd Place

2004: Liberal over Conservative by 13,895 votes, 29% of votes cast.
2006: Liberal over Conservative by 11,026 votes, 21% of votes cast.
2008: Liberal over Conservative by 7,934 votes, 17% of votes cast.
2011: Conservative over Liberal by 1,207 votes, 2.5% of votes cast.
2015: Liberal over Conservative by 7,166 votes, 12% of votes cast.

Analysis

This riding typically votes Liberal. Their candidates won four of the past five elections, including Election 2015. Voter turnout rose from 61% in 2011 to 69% in 2015.

Renfrew–Nipissing–Pembroke, Electoral District #35086

Recommended Vote to Keep Your Guns

Vote for Conservative incumbent Cheryl Gallant.

History at a Glance: 1st and 2nd Place

2004: Conservative over Liberal by 12,696 votes, 25% of votes cast.
2006: Conservative over Liberal by 17,391 votes, 34% of votes cast.
2008: Conservative over Liberal by 19,171 votes, 41% of votes cast.
2011: Conservative over Liberal by 17,851 votes, 35% of votes cast.
2015: Conservative over Liberal by 7,529 votes, 13% of votes cast.

Analysis

Conservative incumbent Cheryl Gallant has won this electoral district in every election since 2000.

Voter turnout rose from 66% in 2011 to 72% in 2015.

Richmond Hill, Electoral District #35087

Recommended Vote to Keep Your Guns

Vote Conservative.

History at a Glance: 1st and 2nd Place

2004: Liberal over Conservative by 15,572 votes, 34% of votes cast.
2006: Liberal over Conservative by 11,273 votes, 22% of votes cast.
2008: Liberal over Conservative by 5,170 votes, 11% of votes cast.
2011: Conservative over Liberal by 4,407 votes, 8.8% of votes cast.
2015: Liberal over Conservative by 1,757 votes, 3.6% of votes cast.

Analysis

This riding typically votes Liberal. Their candidates won four of the past five elections, including Election 2015. Voter turnout rose from 55% in 2011 to 61% in 2015.

Sarnia–Lambton, Electoral District #35091

Recommended Vote to Keep Your Guns

Vote for Conservative incumbent Marilyn Gladu.

History at a Glance: 1st and 2nd Place

2004: Liberal over Conservative by 5,432 votes, 11% of votes cast.
2006: Conservative over Liberal by 4,192 votes, 7.9% of votes cast.
2008: Conservative over NDP by 13,158 votes, 28% of votes cast.
2011: Conservative over NDP by 11,256 votes, 23% of votes cast.
2015: Conservative over NDP by 4,463 votes, 7.7% of votes cast.

Analysis

This riding typically votes Conservative. Their candidates won four of the past five elections, including Election 2015. Voter turnout rose from 62% in 2011 to 71% in 2015.

Sault Ste. Marie, Electoral District #35092

Recommended Vote to Keep Your Guns

Vote Conservative.

History at a Glance: 1st and 2nd Place

2004: NDP over Liberal by 752 votes, 1.7% of votes cast.
2006: NDP over Liberal by 2,154 votes, 4.7% of votes cast.
2008: NDP over Conservative by 1,111 votes, 2.7% of votes cast.
2011: Conservative over NDP by 1,861 votes, 4.2% of votes cast.
2015: Liberal over Conservative by 5,967 votes, 14% of votes cast.

Analysis

Election 2015 was the first win for Liberals in the past five elections. Voter turnout rose from 64% in 2011 to 68% in 2015.

Scarborough Centre, Electoral District #35094

Recommended Vote to Keep Your Guns

Vote Conservative.

History at a Glance: 1st and 2nd Place

2004: Liberal over Conservative by 12,225 votes, 33% of votes cast.
2006: Liberal over Conservative by 11,810 votes, 28% of votes cast.
2008: Liberal over Conservative by 6,839 votes, 19% of votes cast.
2011: Conservative over Liberal by 1,470 votes, 3.9% of votes cast.
2015: Liberal over Conservative by 8,048 votes, 18% of votes cast.

Analysis

This riding typically votes Liberal. Their candidates won four of the past five elections, including Election 2015. Voter turnout rose from 54% in 2011 to 63% in 2015.

Scarborough North, Electoral District #35096

Recommended Vote to Keep Your Guns

Vote Conservative.

History at a Glance: 1st and 2nd Place

2004: Liberal over Independent by 15,602 votes, 40% of votes cast.
2006: Liberal over Conservative by 20,853 votes, 45% of votes cast.
2008: Liberal over Conservative by 14,558 votes, 36% of votes cast.
2011: NDP over Conservative by 5,000 votes, 11% of votes cast.
2015: Liberal over Conservative by 8,167 votes, 21% of votes cast.

Analysis

This riding typically votes Liberal. Their candidates won four of the past five elections, including Election 2015. Voter turnout rose from 55% in 2011 to 60% in 2015.

Scarborough Southwest, Electoral District #35098

Recommended Vote to Keep Your Guns

Vote for Conservative candidate Kimberly Fawcett.

History at a Glance: 1st and 2nd Place

2004: Liberal over Conservative by 9,748 votes, 26% of votes cast.
2006: Liberal over Conservative by 9,913 votes, 24% of votes cast.
2008: Liberal over Conservative by 4,558 votes, 12% of votes cast.
2011: NDP over Conservative by 1,289 votes, 3.2% of votes cast.
2015: Liberal over NDP by 14,012 votes, 29% of votes cast.

Analysis

The Liberal incumbent promotes gun bans and is a candidate to send into retirement in Election 2019.

The Conservative candidate, Kimberly Fawcett, is a decorated officer in the Canadian Armed Forces.

Voter turnout rose from 58% in 2011 to 66% in 2015.

Scarborough–Agincourt, Electoral District #35093

Recommended Vote to Keep Your Guns

Vote Conservative.

History at a Glance: 1st and 2nd Place

2004: Liberal over Conservative by 17,751 votes, 43% of votes cast.
2006: Liberal over Conservative by 17,381 votes, 39% of votes cast.
2008: Liberal over Conservative by 10,959 votes, 27% of votes cast.
2011: Liberal over Conservative by 4,568 votes, 11% of votes cast.
2014 By-Election: Liberal over Conservative by 6,524 votes, or 30% of votes cast.
2015: Liberal over Conservative by 5,785 votes, 14% of votes cast.
2017 By-Election: Liberal over Conservative by 1,630 votes, 8.9% of votes cast.

Analysis

Liberals won the past seven elections. Voter turnout rose from 56% in 2011 to 59% in 2015.

Scarborough–Guildwood, Electoral District #35095

Recommended Vote to Keep Your Guns

Vote Conservative.

History at a Glance: 1st and 2nd Place

2004: Liberal over Conservative by 12,673 votes, 35% of votes cast.
2006: Liberal over Conservative by 10,087 votes, 25% of votes cast.
2008: Liberal over Conservative by 7,217 votes, 20% of votes cast.
2011: Liberal over Conservative by 691 votes, 1.8% of votes cast.
2015: Liberal over Conservative by 14,059 votes, 34% of votes cast.

Analysis

This riding typically votes Liberal. Their candidates won the past five elections. Voter turnout rose from 56% in 2011 to 64% in 2015.

Scarborough–Rouge Park, Electoral District #35097

Recommended Vote to Keep Your Guns

Vote Conservative.

History at a Glance: 1st and 2nd Place

2015: Liberal over Conservative by 16,326 votes, 33% of votes cast.

Analysis

This electoral district was created prior to the 2015 federal election.

Simcoe North, Electoral District #35100

Recommended Vote to Keep Your Guns

Vote for Conservative incumbent Bruce Stanton.

History at a Glance: 1st and 2nd Place

2004: Liberal over Conservative by 3,094 votes, 5.7% of votes cast.
2006: Conservative over Liberal by 1,188 votes, 2.1% of votes cast.
2008: Conservative over Liberal by 11,658 votes, 22% of votes cast.
2011: Conservative over NDP by 20,066 votes, 35% of votes cast.
2015: Conservative over Liberal by 2,118 votes, 3.7% of votes cast.

Analysis

This riding typically votes Conservative. Their candidates won four of the past five elections, including Election 2015. Voter turnout rose from 64% in 2011 to 66% in 2015.

Simcoe–Grey, Electoral District #35099

Recommended Vote to Keep Your Guns

Vote Conservative.

History at a Glance: 1st and 2nd Place

2004: Conservative over Liberal by 100 votes, 0.2% of votes cast.
2006: Conservative over Liberal by 11,446 votes, 19% of votes cast.
2008: Conservative over Liberal by 18,798 votes, 33% of votes cast.
2011: Conservative over NDP by 20,599 votes, 32% of votes cast.
2015: Conservative over Liberal by 5,260 votes, 8.0% of votes cast.

Analysis

This riding typically votes Conservative. Their candidates won the past five elections. Voter turnout rose from 65% in 2011 to 67% in 2015.

Spadina–Fort York, Electoral District #35101

Recommended Vote to Keep Your Guns

Vote NDP because they are your best choice to defeat the Liberals.

History at a Glance: 1st and 2nd Place

2004: Liberal over NDP by 805 votes, 1.4% of votes cast.
2006: NDP over Liberal by 3,681 votes, 5.9% of votes cast.
2008: NDP over Liberal by 3,484 votes, 5.8% of votes cast.
2011: NDP over Liberal by 20,325 votes, 31% of votes cast.
2014 By-Election: Liberal over NDP by 6,745 votes, or 19% of votes.
2015: Liberal over NDP by 15,094 votes, 27% of votes cast.

Analysis

The battle here is between Liberal and NDP. Voter turnout rose from 65% in 2011 to 69% in 2015 and elected an activist against gun owners.

St. Catharines, Electoral District #35089

Recommended Vote to Keep Your Guns

Vote Conservative.

History at a Glance: 1st and 2nd Place

2004: Liberal over Conservative by 3,016 votes, 5.7% of votes cast.
2006: Conservative over Liberal by 246 votes, 0.4% of votes cast.
2008: Conservative over Liberal by 8,822 votes, 17% of votes cast.
2011: Conservative over NDP by 13,598 votes, 27% of votes cast.
2015: Liberal over Conservative by 3,233 votes, 5.6% of votes cast.

Analysis

This riding tends to vote Conservative, winning three of the past five elections. Voter turnout rose from 60% in 2011 to 67% in 2015.

Stormont–Dundas–South Glengarry, Electoral District #35102

Recommended Vote to Keep Your Guns

Vote Conservative.

History at a Glance: 1st and 2nd Place

2004: Conservative over Liberal by 3,899 votes, 8.1% of votes cast.
2006: Conservative over Liberal by 14,108 votes, 28% of votes cast.
2008: Conservative over Liberal by 17,292 votes, 38% of votes cast.
2011: Conservative over Liberal by 21,028 votes, 44% of votes cast.
2015: Conservative over Liberal by 6,639 votes, 13% of votes cast.

Analysis

This riding typically votes Conservative and Guy Lauzon has won the past five elections. Voter turnout rose from 62% in 2011 to 67% in 2015.

Lauzon said he will not run again in 2019.

Sudbury, Electoral District #35103

Recommended Vote to Keep Your Guns

Vote NDP because they are your best choice to defeat the Liberals.

History at a Glance: 1st and 2nd Place

2004: Liberal over NDP by 6,133 votes, 14% of votes cast.
2006: Liberal over NDP by 4,584 votes, 9.6% of votes cast.
2008: NDP over Liberal by 2,125 votes, 4.9% of votes cast.
2011: NDP over Conservative by 9,803 votes, 22% of votes cast.
2015: Liberal over NDP by 9,741 votes, 20% of votes cast.

Analysis

Liberals won three of the past five elections, including Election 2015. Voter turnout rose from 63% in 2011 to 68% in 2015.

Thornhill, Electoral District #35104

Recommended Vote to Keep Your Guns

Vote for Conservative incumbent Peter Kent.

History at a Glance: 1st and 2nd Place

2004: Liberal over Conservative by 10,584 votes, 20% of votes cast.
2006: Liberal over Conservative by 10,929 votes, 19% of votes cast.
2008: Conservative over Liberal by 5,212 votes, 9.6% of votes cast.
2011: Conservative over Liberal by 22,504 votes, 38% of votes cast.
2015: Conservative over Liberal by 13,516 votes, 25% of votes cast.

Analysis

This riding tends to vote Conservative. Their candidates won three of the past five elections, including Election 2015. Voter turnout rose from 60% in 2011 to 67% in 2015.

Thunder Bay–Rainy River, Electoral District #35105

Recommended Vote to Keep Your Guns

Vote NDP because they are your best choice to defeat the Liberals.

History at a Glance: 1st and 2nd Place

2004: Liberal over NDP by 3,509 votes, 9.7% of votes cast.
2006: Liberal over NDP by 658 votes, 1.7% of votes cast.
2008: NDP over Liberal by 2,895 votes, 8.1% of votes cast.
2011: NDP over Conservative by 7,994 votes, 22% of votes cast.
2015: Liberal over NDP by 6,024 votes, 14% of votes cast.

Analysis

This riding tends to vote Liberal. Their candidates won three of the past five elections, including Election 2015. Voter turnout rose from 59% in 2011 to 66% in 2015.

Thunder Bay–Superior North, Electoral District #35106

Recommended Vote to Keep Your Guns

Vote NDP because they are your best choice to defeat the Liberals.

History at a Glance: 1st and 2nd Place

2004: Liberal over NDP by 4,792 votes, 14% of votes cast.
2006: Liberal over NDP by 408 votes, 1.0% of votes cast.
2008: NDP over Liberal by 3,104 votes, 8.7% of votes cast.
2011: NDP over Conservative by 7,440 votes, 20% of votes cast.
2015: Liberal over NDP by 9,730 votes, 22% of votes cast.

Analysis

This riding tends to vote Liberal and NDP. Liberal candidates won three of the past five elections, including Election 2015 and the NDP won both 2008 and 2011. Voter turnout rose from 60% in 2011 to 68% in 2015.

Timmins–James Bay, Electoral District #35107

Recommended Vote to Keep Your Guns

Vote for NDP incumbent Charlie Angus.

History at a Glance: 1st and 2nd Place

2004: NDP over Liberal by 613 votes, 1.8% of votes cast.
2006: NDP over Liberal by 6,192 votes, 16% of votes cast.
2008: NDP over Liberal by 10,448 votes, 34% of votes cast.
2011: NDP over Conservative by 6,212 votes, 19% of votes cast.
2015: NDP over Liberal by 3,034 votes, 8.1% of votes cast.

Analysis

This riding typically votes NDP. Their candidates won the past five elections. Voter turnout rose from 55% in 2011 to 61% in 2015.

Toronto Centre, Electoral District #35108

Recommended Vote to Keep Your Guns

Vote NDP because they are your best choice to defeat the Liberals.

History at a Glance: 1st and 2nd Place

2004: Liberal over NDP by 17,589 votes, 33% of votes cast.
2006: Liberal over NDP by 16,838 votes, 28% of votes cast.
2008: Liberal over Conservative by 18,060 votes, 35% of votes cast.
2011: Liberal over NDP by 6,014 votes, 11% of votes cast.
2013 By-Election: Liberal over NDP by 4,554 votes, 13% of votes cast.
2015: Liberal over NDP by 15,830 votes, 31% of votes cast.

Analysis

This riding typically votes Liberal. Their candidates won the past five elections. Voter turnout rose from 63% in 2011 to 69% in 2015.

188 · A MANUAL FOR POLITICAL ACTION

Toronto–Danforth, Electoral District #35109

Recommended Vote to Keep Your Guns

Vote NDP because they are your best choice to defeat the Liberals.

History at a Glance: 1st and 2nd Place

2004: NDP over Liberal by 2,395 votes, 5.0% of votes cast.
2006: NDP over Liberal by 7,156 votes, 14% of votes cast.
2008: NDP over Liberal by 6,987 votes, 15% of votes cast.
2011: NDP over Liberal by 20,763 votes, 43% of votes cast.
2012 By-Election: NDP over Liberal by 9,995 votes, 31% of votes cast.
2015: Liberal over NDP by 1,206 votes, 2.2% of votes cast.

Analysis

Election 2015 was the first win for Liberals in the past six elections. Voter turnout rose from 65% in 2011 to 71% in 2015.

Toronto–St. Paul's, Electoral District #35090

Recommended Vote to Keep Your Guns

Vote Conservative.

History at a Glance: 1st and 2nd Place

2004: Liberal over Conservative by 20,945 votes, 38% of votes cast.
2006: Liberal over Conservative by 14,274 votes, 24% of votes cast.
2008: Liberal over Conservative by 12,338 votes, 24% of votes cast.
2011: Liberal over Conservative by 4,545 votes, 8.2% of votes cast.
2015: Liberal over Conservative by 16,105 votes, 28% of votes cast.

Analysis

This riding typically votes Liberal and Carolyn Bennett has won the past five elections. Voter turnout rose from 66% in 2011 to 72% in 2015.

University–Rosedale, Electoral District #35110

Recommended Vote to Keep Your Guns

Vote NDP because they are your best choice to defeat the Liberals.

History at a Glance: 1st and 2nd Place

2015: Liberal over NDP by 11,861 votes, 22% of votes cast.

Analysis

This electoral district was created prior to the 2015 federal election and voters in this area typically support NDP candidates.

Vaughan–Woodbridge, Electoral District #35111

Recommended Vote to Keep Your Guns

Vote Conservative.

History at a Glance: 1st and 2nd Place

2004: Liberal over Conservative by 19,609 votes, 39% of votes cast.
2006: Liberal over Conservative by 20,844 votes, 34% of votes cast.
2008: Liberal over Conservative by 8,383 votes, 15% of votes cast.
2011: Conservative over Liberal by 18,098 votes, 26% of votes cast.
2015: Liberal over Conservative by 2,295 votes, 4.9% of votes cast.

Analysis

This riding typically votes Liberal. Their candidates won four of the past five elections, including Election 2015. Voter turnout rose from 55% in 2011 to 63% in 2015.

Waterloo, Electoral District #35112

Recommended Vote to Keep Your Guns

Vote Conservative.

History at a Glance: 1st and 2nd Place

2004: Liberal over Conservative by 10,860 votes, 19% of votes cast.
2006: Liberal over Conservative by 12,319 votes, 19% of votes cast.
2008: Conservative over Liberal by 17 votes, 0.02% of votes cast.
2011: Conservative over Liberal by 2,144 votes, 3.2% of votes cast.
2015: Liberal over Conservative by 10,434 votes, 17% of votes cast.

Analysis

This riding tends to vote Liberal. Their candidates won three of the past five elections. Voter turnout rose from 68.97% in 2011 to 73.00% in 2015.

Wellington–Halton Hills, Electoral District #35113

Recommended Vote to Keep Your Guns

Vote for Conservative incumbent Michael Chong.

History at a Glance: 1st and 2nd Place

2004: Conservative over Liberal by 2,306 votes, 4.6% of votes cast.
2006: Conservative over Liberal by 11,842 votes, 21% of votes cast.
2008: Conservative over Liberal by 17,879 votes, 35% of votes cast.
2011: Conservative over Liberal by 26,098 votes, 47% of votes cast.
2015: Conservative over Liberal by 9,203 votes, 14% of votes cast.

Analysis

This riding typically votes Conservative and Michael Chong won the past five elections. Voter turnout rose from 66% in 2011 to 71% in 2015.

Whitby, Electoral District #35114

Recommended Vote to Keep Your Guns

Vote Conservative.

History at a Glance: 1st and 2nd Place

2004: Liberal over Conservative by 5,118 votes, 9.0% of votes cast.
2006: Conservative over Liberal by 3,412 votes, 5.1% of votes cast.
2008: Conservative over Liberal by 15,244 votes, 25% of votes cast.
2011: Conservative over NDP by 23,220 votes, 36% of votes cast.
2014 By-Election: Conservative over Liberal by 2,999 votes, or 8.7% of votes cast.
2015: Liberal over Conservative by 1,849 votes, 2.9% of votes cast.

Analysis

This riding tends to vote Conservative. Their candidates won three of the past five elections. Voter turnout rose from 62% in 2011 to 70% in 2015. The first-term Liberal incumbent will not seek re-election, opening the door for the Conservative Party to regain this seat.

Willowdale, Electoral District #35115

Recommended Vote to Keep Your Guns

Vote Conservative.

History at a Glance: 1st and 2nd Place

2004: Liberal over Conservative by 19,240 votes, 38% of votes cast.
2006: Liberal over Conservative by 14,369 votes, 26% of votes cast.
2008: Liberal over Conservative by 7,958 votes, 16% of votes cast.
2011: Conservative over Liberal by 932 votes, 1.7% of votes cast.
2015: Liberal over Conservative by 7,529 votes, 16% of votes cast.

Analysis

This riding typically votes Liberal. Their candidates won four of the past five elections, including Election 2015. Voter turnout rose from 57% in 2011 to 60% in 2015.

Windsor West, Electoral District #35117

Recommended Vote to Keep Your Guns

Vote for NDP incumbent Brian Masse.

History at a Glance: 1st and 2nd Place

2004: NDP over Liberal by 6,466 votes, 15% of votes cast.
2006: NDP over Liberal by 11,498 votes, 24% of votes cast.
2008: NDP over Conservative by 11,837 votes, 30% of votes cast.
2011: NDP over Conservative by 9,015 votes, 23% of votes cast.
2015: NDP over Liberal by 12,243 votes, 26% of votes cast.

Analysis

This riding typically votes NDP and Brian Masse won the past five elections. Voter turnout rose from 48% in 2011 to 54% in 2015.

Windsor–Tecumseh, Electoral District #35116

Recommended Vote to Keep Your Guns

Vote for NDP incumbent Cheryl Hardcastle.

History at a Glance: 1st and 2nd Place

2004: NDP over Liberal by 3,818 votes, 8.0% of votes cast.
2006: NDP over Liberal by 9,233 votes, 18% of votes cast.
2008: NDP over Conservative by 10,638 votes, 25% of votes cast.
2011: NDP over Conservative by 7,290 votes, 16% of votes cast.
2015: NDP over Conservative by 8,559 votes, 16% of votes cast.

Analysis

This riding typically votes NDP. Their candidates won the past five elections. Voter turnout rose from 53% in 2011 to 61% in 2015.

York Centre, Electoral District #35118

Recommended Vote to Keep Your Guns

Vote Conservative.

History at a Glance: 1st and 2nd Place

2004: Liberal over Conservative by 11,202 votes, 29% of votes cast.
2006: Liberal over Conservative by 9,640 votes, 23% of votes cast.
2008: Liberal over Conservative by 2,032 votes, 5.5% of votes cast.
2011: Conservative over Liberal by 6,377 votes, 15% of votes cast.
2015: Liberal over Conservative by 1,238 votes, 2.9% of votes cast.

Analysis

This riding typically votes Liberal. Their candidates won four of the past five elections, including Election 2015. Voter turnout rose from 58% in 2011 to 65% in 2015.

York South–Weston, Electoral District #35120

Recommended Vote to Keep Your Guns

Vote NDP because they are your best choice to defeat the Liberals.

History at a Glance: 1st and 2nd Place

2004: Liberal over NDP by 13,256 votes, 39% of votes cast.
2006: Liberal over NDP by 14,346 votes, 36% of votes cast.
2008: Liberal over NDP by 6,430 votes, 19% of votes cast.
2011: NDP over Liberal by 2,580 votes, 7.3% of votes cast.
2015: Liberal over NDP by 6,812 votes, 16% of votes cast.

Analysis

This riding typically votes Liberal. Their candidates won four of the past five elections, including Election 2015. Voter turnout rose from 51% in 2011 to 61% in 2015.

York–Simcoe, Electoral District #35119

Recommended Vote to Keep Your Guns

Vote for Conservative incumbent Scot Davidson.

History at a Glance: 1st and 2nd Place

2004: Conservative over Liberal by 4,580 votes, 9.7% of votes cast.
2006: Conservative over Liberal by 9,229 votes, 17% of votes cast.
2008: Conservative over Liberal by 18,368 votes, 38% of votes cast.
2011: Conservative over NDP by 23,424 votes, 44% of votes cast.
2015: Conservative over Liberal by 5,975 votes, 12% of votes cast.
2019 By-Election: Conservative over Liberal by 4,118 votes, or 25% of votes cast.

Analysis

This riding typically votes Conservative. Voter turnout rose from 58% in 2011 to 63% in 2015.

Manitoba

Brandon–Souris, Electoral District #46001

Recommended Vote to Keep Your Guns

Vote Conservative.

History at a Glance: 1st and 2nd Place

2004: Conservative over Liberal by 9,687 votes, 28% of votes cast.
2006: Conservative over NDP by 12,719 votes, 34% of votes cast.
2008: Conservative over NDP by 13,503 votes, 39% of votes cast.
2011: Conservative over NDP by 13,541 votes, 39% of votes cast.
2013 By-Election: Conservative over Liberal by 389 votes, or 1.4% of votes cast.
2015: Conservative over Liberal by 5,328 votes, 13% of votes cast.

Analysis

Conservatives won the past six elections. Incumbent Larry Maguire is not running again in 2019. Voter turnout rose from 57% in 2011 to 67% in 2015.

Charleswood–St. James–Assiniboia–Headingley, Electoral District #46002

Recommended Vote to Keep Your Guns

Vote Conservative.

History at a Glance: 1st and 2nd Place

2004: Conservative over Liberal by 734 votes, 1.7% of votes cast.
2006: Conservative over Liberal by 4,692 votes, 11% of votes cast.
2008: Conservative over Liberal by 13,074 votes, 33% of votes cast.
2011: Conservative over NDP by 15,130 votes, 37% of votes cast.
2015: Liberal over Conservative by 6,123 votes, 13% of votes cast.

Analysis

This riding tends to vote Conservative, who won four of the past five elections. Voter turnout rose from 65% in 2011 to 74% in 2015.

Churchill–Keewatinook Aski, Electoral District #46003

Recommended Vote to Keep Your Guns

Vote for NDP incumbent Niki Ashton.

History at a Glance: 1st and 2nd Place

2004: NDP over Liberal by 1,008 votes, 5.1% of votes cast.
2006: Liberal over NDP by 3,064 votes, 12% of votes cast.
2008: NDP over Liberal by 3,445 votes, 19% of votes cast.
2011: NDP over Conservative by 5,006 votes, 25% of votes cast.
2015: NDP over Liberal by 912 votes, 3.0% of votes cast.

Analysis

Voter turnout rose from 44% in 2011 to 58% in 2015 in a riding that typically votes NDP.

Dauphin–Swan River–Neepawa, Electoral District #46004

Recommended Vote to Keep Your Guns

Vote Conservative.

History at a Glance: 1st and 2nd Place

2004: Conservative over NDP by 10,684 votes, 32% of votes cast.
2006: Conservative over NDP by 13,863 votes, 41% of votes cast.
2008: Conservative over NDP by 13,218 votes, 45% of votes cast.
2011: Conservative over NDP by 10,886 votes, 37% of votes cast.
2015: Conservative over Liberal by 7,000 votes, 17% of votes cast.

Analysis

This riding tends to vote Conservative. Their candidates won the past five elections. Voter turnout rose from 55% in 2011 to 65% in 2015.

Conservative incumbent Robert Sopuck will not run again in 2019.

Elmwood–Transcona, Electoral District #46005

Recommended Vote to Keep Your Guns

Vote Conservative.

History at a Glance: 1st and 2nd Place

2004: NDP over Conservative by 7,577 votes, 26% of votes cast.
2006: NDP over Conservative by 6,247 votes, 19% of votes cast.
2008: NDP over Conservative by 1,579 votes, 5.0% of votes cast.
2011: Conservative over NDP by 300 votes, 0.9% of votes cast.
2015: NDP over Conservative by 61 votes, 0.1% of votes cast.

Analysis

This riding tends to vote NDP. Their candidates won four of the past five elections, including Election 2015. Voter turnout rose from 56% in 2011 to 65% in 2015.

This is a seat the Conservative Party can and should win in 2019.

Kildonan–St. Paul, Electoral District #46006

Recommended Vote to Keep Your Guns

Vote Conservative.

History at a Glance: 1st and 2nd Place

2004: Conservative over Liberal by 278 votes, 0.8% of votes cast.
2006: Conservative over Liberal by 3,927 votes, 9.7% of votes cast.
2008: Conservative over NDP by 7,658 votes, 21% of votes cast.
2011: Conservative over NDP by 10,943 votes, 28% of votes cast.
2015: Liberal over Conservative by 1,239 votes, 2.8% of votes cast.

Analysis

Election 2015 was the first win for the Liberals in the past five elections. This riding tends to vote Conservative. Their candidates won four of the past five elections. Voter turnout rose from 61% in 2011 to 70% in 2015.

Portage–Lisgar, Electoral District #46007

Recommended Vote to Keep Your Guns

Vote for Conservative incumbent Candice Bergen.

History at a Glance: 1st and 2nd Place

2004: Conservative over Liberal by 16,765 votes, 48% of votes cast.
2006: Conservative over Liberal by 21,520 votes, 58% of votes cast.
2008: Conservative over Liberal by 17,662 votes, 55% of votes cast.
2011: Conservative over NDP by 23,421 votes, 66% of votes cast.
2015: Conservative over Liberal by 14,439 votes, 35% of votes cast.

Analysis

This riding tends to vote Conservative. Their candidates won the past five elections. Voter turnout rose from 59% in 2011 to 65% in 2015.

Provencher, Electoral District #46008

Recommended Vote to Keep Your Guns

Vote for Conservative incumbent Ted Falk.

History at a Glance: 1st and 2nd Place

2004: Conservative over Liberal by 13,719 votes, 38% of votes cast.
2006: Conservative over Liberal by 19,122 votes, 50% of votes cast.
2008: Conservative over NDP by 18,356 votes, 51% of votes cast.
2011: Conservative over NDP by 20,769 votes, 53% of votes cast.
2013 By-Election: Conservative over Liberal by 6,335 votes, or 28% of votes cast.
2015: Conservative over Liberal by 9,577 votes, 21% of votes cast.

Analysis

This riding tends to vote Conservative. Their candidates won the past six elections. Voter turnout rose from 61% in 2011 to 68% in 2015.

Saint Boniface–Saint Vital, Electoral District #46009

Recommended Vote to Keep Your Guns

Vote Conservative.

History at a Glance: 1st and 2nd Place

2004: Liberal over Conservative by 6,033 votes, 16% of votes cast.
2006: Liberal over Conservative by 1,524 votes, 3.6% of votes cast.
2008: Conservative over Liberal by 4,712 votes, 11% of votes cast.
2011: Conservative over Liberal by 8,423 votes, 19% of votes cast.
2015: Liberal over Conservative by 14,525 votes, 30% of votes cast.

Analysis

This riding tends to vote Liberal. Their candidates won three of the past five elections, including Election 2015. Voter turnout rose from 66% in 2011 to 74% in 2015.

Selkirk–Interlake–Eastman, Electoral District #46010

Recommended Vote to Keep Your Guns

Vote for Conservative incumbent James Bezan.

History at a Glance: 1st and 2nd Place

2004: Conservative over NDP by 8,211 votes, 21% of votes cast.
2006: Conservative over NDP by 5,303 votes, 12% of votes cast.
2008: Conservative over NDP by 13,796 votes, 36% of votes cast.
2011: Conservative over NDP by 15,915 votes, 39% of votes cast.
2015: Conservative over Liberal by 10,109 votes, 20% of votes cast.

Analysis

This riding tends to vote Conservative. Their candidates won the past five elections. Voter turnout rose from 62% in 2011 to 68% in 2015.

Winnipeg Centre, Electoral District #46011

Recommended Vote to Keep Your Guns

Vote NDP because they are your best choice to defeat the Liberals.

History at a Glance: 1st and 2nd Place

2004: NDP over Liberal by 2,864 votes, 11% of votes cast.
2006: NDP over Liberal by 6,865 votes, 24% of votes cast.
2008: NDP over Conservative by 6,848 votes, 27% of votes cast.
2011: NDP over Conservative by 6,755 votes, 26% of votes cast.
2015: Liberal over NDP by 8,981 votes, 27% of votes cast.

Analysis

Election 2015 was the first win for the Liberals in the past five elections. This riding tends to vote NDP and they won the four elections prior to 2015. Voter turnout rose from 48% in 2011 to 59% in 2015.

Winnipeg North, Electoral District #46012

Recommended Vote to Keep Your Guns

Vote Conservative.

History at a Glance: 1st and 2nd Place

2004: NDP over Liberal by 3,016 votes, 12% of votes cast.
2006: NDP over Liberal by 9,830 votes, 36% of votes cast.
2008: NDP over Conservative by 9,064 votes, 40% of votes cast.
2011: Liberal over NDP by 44 votes, 0.2% of votes cast.
2015: Liberal over Conservative by 18,209 votes, 54% of votes cast.

Analysis

NDP won three of the past five elections and only narrowly lost in 2011. Voter turnout rose from 49% in 2011 to 58% in 2015.

Winnipeg South, Electoral District #46013

Recommended Vote to Keep Your Guns

Vote Conservative.

History at a Glance: 1st and 2nd Place

2004: Liberal over Conservative by 6,500 votes, 17% of votes cast.
2006: Conservative over Liberal by 111 votes, 0.3% of votes cast.
2008: Conservative over Liberal by 5,733 votes, 14% of votes cast.
2011: Conservative over Liberal by 8,544 votes, 20% of votes cast.
2015: Liberal over Conservative by 11,387 votes, 24% of votes cast.

Analysis

This riding tends to vote Conservative. Their candidates won three of the past five elections. This riding elected Liberal candidates in two of the past five elections, including Election 2015, which they won by 11,387 votes. Voter turnout rose from 68% in 2011 to 75% in 2015.

Winnipeg South Centre, Electoral District #46014

Recommended Vote to Keep Your Guns

Vote Conservative.

History at a Glance: 1st and 2nd Place

2004: Liberal over Conservative by 7,617 votes, 20% of votes cast.
2006: Liberal over Conservative by 3,219 votes, 7.8% of votes cast.
2008: Liberal over Conservative by 2,335 votes, 6.0% of votes cast.
2011: Conservative over Liberal by 722 votes, 1.8% of votes cast.
2015: Liberal over Conservative by 16,891 votes, 32% of votes cast.

Analysis

This riding tends to vote Liberal. Their candidates won four of the past five elections, including Election 2015. Voter turnout rose from 69% in 2011 to 76% in 2015.

Saskatchewan

Battlefords–Lloydminster, Electoral District #47001

Recommended Vote to Keep Your Guns

Vote for Conservative incumbent Rosemarie Ashley Falk.

History at a Glance: 1st and 2nd Place

2004: Conservative over NDP by 10,074 votes, 38% of votes cast.
2006: Conservative over NDP by 11,662 votes, 38% of votes cast.
2008: Conservative over NDP by 9,049 votes, 35% of votes cast.
2011: Conservative over NDP by 11,436 votes, 40% of votes cast.
2015: Conservative over NDP by 14,617 votes, 43% of votes cast.
2017 By-Election: Conservative over NDP by 7,254 votes, or 56% of votes cast.

Analysis

This riding tends to vote Conservative. Their candidates won the past six elections. Voter turnout rose from 57% in 2011 to 66% in 2015.

Carlton Trail–Eagle Creek, Electoral District #47004

Recommended Vote to Keep Your Guns

Vote for Conservative incumbent Kelly Block.

History at a Glance: 1st and 2nd Place

2004: Conservative over Liberal by 4,556 votes, 14% of votes cast.
2006: Conservative over Liberal by 9,098 votes, 25% of votes cast.
2008: Conservative over NDP by 10,422 votes, 32% of votes cast.
2011: Conservative over NDP by 9,788 votes, 27% of votes cast.
2015: Conservative over NDP by 18,505 votes, 46% of votes cast.

Analysis

This riding tends to vote Conservative. Their candidates won the past five elections. Voter turnout rose from 63% in 2011 to 72% in 2015.

Cypress Hills–Grasslands, Electoral District #47002

Recommended Vote to Keep Your Guns

Vote Conservative.

History at a Glance: 1st and 2nd Place

2004: Conservative over Liberal by 12,463 votes, 42% of votes cast.
2006: Conservative over NDP by 14,959 votes, 50% of votes cast.
2008: Conservative over NDP by 13,528 votes, 49% of votes cast.
2011: Conservative over NDP by 14,307 votes, 49% of votes cast.
2015: Conservative over Liberal by 19,669 votes, 54% of votes cast.

Analysis

This riding tends to vote Conservative. Their candidates won the past five elections. Voter turnout rose from 66% in 2011 to 71% in 2015.

Conservative incumbent David Anderson will not run again in 2019.

Desnethé–Missinippi–Churchill River, Electoral District #47003

Recommended Vote to Keep Your Guns

Vote Conservative.

History at a Glance: 1st and 2nd Place

2004: Conservative over Liberal by 1,464 votes, 7.5% of votes cast.
2006: Liberal over Conservative by 67 votes, 0.3% of votes cast.
2008: Conservative over Liberal by 3,148 votes, 16% of votes cast.
2011: Conservative over NDP by 794 votes, 3.6% of votes cast.
2015: NDP over Liberal by 82 votes, 0.3% of votes cast.

Analysis

Conservatives won three of the past five elections, then fell to third place in 2015. Voter turnout rose from 50% in 2011 to 65% in 2015.

Moose Jaw–Lake Centre–Lanigan, Electoral District #47005

Recommended Vote to Keep Your Guns

Vote for Conservative incumbent Tom Lukiwski.

History at a Glance: 1st and 2nd Place

2004: Conservative over NDP by 124 votes, 0.4% of votes cast.
2006: Conservative over NDP by 3,446 votes, 9.9% of votes cast.
2008: Conservative over NDP by 3,294 votes, 10% of votes cast.
2011: Conservative over NDP by 766 votes, 2.3% of votes cast.
2015: Conservative over NDP by 13,295 votes, 32% of votes cast.

Analysis

This riding tends to vote Conservative. Their candidates won the past five elections. Voter turnout rose from 67% in 2011 to 72% in 2015.

Prince Albert, Electoral District #47006

Recommended Vote to Keep Your Guns

Vote for Conservative incumbent Randy Hoback.

History at a Glance: 1st and 2nd Place

2004: Conservative over NDP by 6,355 votes, 22% of votes cast.
2006: Conservative over NDP by 9,709 votes, 31% of votes cast.
2008: Conservative over NDP by 8,299 votes, 29% of votes cast.
2011: Conservative over NDP by 9,373 votes, 30% of votes cast.
2015: Conservative over NDP by 8,429 votes, 21% of votes cast.

Analysis

This riding tends to vote Conservative. Their candidates won the past five elections. Voter turnout rose from 60% in 2011 to 68% in 2015.

Regina–Lewvan, Electoral District #47007

Recommended Vote to Keep Your Guns

Vote Conservative.

History at a Glance: 1st and 2nd Place

2004: Conservative over Liberal by 122 votes, 0.4% of votes cast.
2006: Conservative over NDP by 4,709 votes, 14% of votes cast.
2008: Conservative over NDP by 7,090 votes, 23% of votes cast.
2011: Conservative over NDP by 5,558 votes, 16% of votes cast.
2015: NDP over Conservative by 132 votes, 0.3% of votes cast.

Analysis

This riding tends to vote Conservative. Their candidates won four of the past five elections. Voter turnout rose from 66% in 2011 to 74% in 2015.

Regina–Qu'Appelle, Electoral District #47008

Recommended Vote to Keep Your Guns

Vote for Conservative Party leader Andrew Scheer.

History at a Glance: 1st and 2nd Place

2004: Conservative over NDP by 861 votes, 3.1% of votes cast.
2006: Conservative over NDP by 2,712 votes, 8.8% of votes cast.
2008: Conservative over NDP by 5,369 votes, 20% of votes cast.
2011: Conservative over NDP by 4,477 votes, 15% of votes cast.
2015: Conservative over NDP by 5,342 votes, 14% of votes cast.

Analysis

This electoral district tends to vote Conservative. Andrew Scheer, the man we need to be Prime Minister after Election 2019, has won this riding since 2004. Voter turnout rose from 60% in 2011 to 68% in 2015.

Regina–Wascana, Electoral District #47009

Recommended Vote to Keep Your Guns

Vote Conservative.

History at a Glance: 1st and 2nd Place

2004: Liberal over Conservative by 11,858 votes, 33% of votes cast.
2006: Liberal over Conservative by 8,676 votes, 22% of votes cast.
2008: Liberal over Conservative by 4,230 votes, 11% of votes cast.
2011: Liberal over Conservative by 1,532 votes, 4.0% of votes cast.
2015: Liberal over Conservative by 10,621 votes, 25% of votes cast.

Analysis

The Conservatives are neck and neck with the Liberals in this riding as of late August. This creates a historic opportunity to end Liberal dominance and defeat an incumbent who opposes gun owners. Voter turnout rose from 67% in 2011 to 74% in 2015.

Saskatoon West, Electoral District #47012

Recommended Vote to Keep Your Guns

Vote Conservative.

History at a Glance: 1st and 2nd Place

2004: Conservative over NDP by 2,278 votes, 8.6% of votes cast.
2006: Conservative over NDP by 1,919 votes, 6.6% of votes cast.
2008: Conservative over NDP by 262 votes, 1.0% of votes cast.
2011: Conservative over NDP by 538 votes, 1.8% of votes cast.
2015: NDP over Conservative by 2,520 votes, 6.7% of votes cast.

Analysis

This riding tends to vote Conservative. Their candidates won four of the past five elections. Voter turnout rose from 60% in 2011 to 66% in 2015.

Saskatoon–Grasswood, Electoral District #47010

Recommended Vote to Keep Your Guns

Vote for Conservative incumbent Kevin Waugh.

History at a Glance: 1st and 2nd Place

2004: Conservative over Liberal by 3,793 votes, 10% of votes cast.
2006: Conservative over NDP by 7,054 votes, 17% of votes cast.
2008: Conservative over NDP by 10,871 votes, 28% of votes cast.
2011: Conservative over NDP by 7,511 votes, 18% of votes cast.
2015: Conservative over NDP by 5,257 votes, 11% of votes cast.

Analysis

This riding tends to vote Conservative. Their candidates won the past five elections. Voter turnout rose from 69% in 2011 to 77% in 2015.

Saskatoon–University, Electoral District #47011

Recommended Vote to Keep Your Guns

Vote Conservative.

History at a Glance: 1st and 2nd Place

2004: Conservative over NDP by 417 votes, 1.2% of votes cast.
2006: Conservative over NDP by 7,310 votes, 20% of votes cast.
2008: Conservative over NDP by 8,978 votes, 26% of votes cast.
2011: Conservative over NDP by 6,683 votes, 18% of votes cast.
2015: Conservative over NDP by 4,477 votes, 10.0% of votes cast.

Analysis

This riding tends to vote Conservative. Conservative incumbent Brad Trost, who won the past five elections, is retiring. Voter turnout rose from 66% in 2011 to 77% in 2015.

Souris–Moose Mountain, Electoral District #47013

Recommended Vote to Keep Your Guns

Vote for Conservative incumbent Robert Gordon Kitchen

History at a Glance: 1st and 2nd Place

2004: Conservative over Independent by 2,907 votes, 9.5% of votes cast.
2006: Conservative over Liberal by 13,601 votes, 44% of votes cast.
2008: Conservative over NDP by 14,694 votes, 54% of votes cast.
2011: Conservative over NDP by 16,137 votes, 55% of votes cast.
2015: Conservative over NDP by 21,184 votes, 56% of votes cast.

Analysis

This riding tends to vote Conservative. Their candidates won the past five elections. Voter turnout rose from 62% in 2011 to 71% in 2015.

Yorkton–Melville, Electoral District #47014

Recommended Vote to Keep Your Guns

Vote for Conservative incumbent Cathay Wagantall.

History at a Glance: 1st and 2nd Place

2004: Conservative over NDP by 14,050 votes, 44% of votes cast.
2006: Conservative over NDP by 14,571 votes, 45% of votes cast.
2008: Conservative over NDP by 13,748 votes, 47% of votes cast.
2011: Conservative over NDP by 14,975 votes, 47% of votes cast.
2015: Conservative over NDP by 14,287 votes, 39% of votes cast.

Analysis

This electoral district is the long-time home of former MP Garry Breitkreuz, the man responsible for taking down Canada's so-called long gun registry. Cathay Wagantall took over and won in 2015.

Voter turnout rose from 63% in 2011 to 67% in 2015.

Alberta

Banff–Airdrie, Electoral District 48001

Recommended Vote to Keep Your Guns

Vote for Conservative incumbent Blake Richards.

History at a Glance: 1st and 2nd Place

2004: Conservative over Liberal by 27,366 votes, 58% of votes cast.
2006: Conservative over Green by 33,558 votes, 61% of votes cast.
2008: Conservative over Green by 30,479 votes, 60% of votes cast.
2011: Conservative over NDP by 37,074 votes, 63% of votes cast.
2015: Conservative over Liberal by 24,848 votes, 37% of votes cast.

Analysis

This riding typically votes Conservative and their candidates won the past five elections. Voter turnout rose from 61% in 2011 to 72% in 2015.

Battle River–Crowfoot, Electoral District #48002

Recommended Vote to Keep Your Guns

Vote for Conservative incumbent Kevin Sorenson.

History at a Glance: 1st and 2nd Place

2004: Conservative over Liberal by 34,034 votes, 73% of votes cast.
2006: Conservative over NDP by 39,335 votes, 75% of votes cast.
2008: Conservative over NDP by 35,559 votes, 74% of votes cast.
2011: Conservative over NDP by 39,310 votes, 75% of votes cast.
2015: Conservative over Liberal by 42,047 votes, 72% of votes cast.

Analysis

Voter turnout rose from 59% in 2011 to 72% in 2015. This riding typically votes Conservative. Their candidates won the past five elections.

Bow River, Electoral District #48003

Recommended Vote to Keep Your Guns

Vote for Conservative incumbent Martin Shields.

History at a Glance: 1st and 2nd Place

2015: Conservative over Liberal by 31,861 votes, 64% of votes cast.

Analysis

This was a new riding created prior to the 2015 election.

Calgary Centre, Electoral District #48004

Recommended Vote to Keep Your Guns

Vote Conservative.

History at a Glance: 1st and 2nd Place

2004: Conservative over Liberal by 10,887 votes, 21% of votes cast.
2006: Conservative over Liberal by 19,749 votes, 36% of votes cast.
2008: Conservative over Liberal by 17,683 votes, 38% of votes cast.
2011: Conservative over Liberal by 19,770 votes, 40% of votes cast.
2012 By-Election: Conservative over Liberal by 1,158 votes, 4.2% of votes cast
2015: Liberal over Conservative by 750 votes, 1.2% of votes cast.

Analysis

Voter turnout rose from 55% in 2011 to 70% in 2015. This riding typically votes Conservative and their candidates won five of the past six elections, including the 2012 By-Election.

Calgary Confederation, Electoral District #48005

Recommended Vote to Keep Your Guns

Vote for Conservative incumbent Len Webber.

History at a Glance: 1st and 2nd Place

2004: Conservative over Liberal by 17,050 votes, 33% of votes cast.
2006: Conservative over NDP by 21,833 votes, 25% of votes cast.
2008: Conservative over NDP by 19,948 votes, 41% of votes cast.
2011: Conservative over NDP by 20,395 votes, 41% of votes cast.
2015: Conservative over Liberal by 1,586 votes, 2.4% of votes cast.

Analysis

Voter turnout rose from 59% in 2011 to 73% in 2015. This riding typically votes Conservative. Their candidates won the past five elections.

Calgary Forest Lawn, Electoral District #48006

Recommended Vote to Keep Your Guns

Vote Conservative

History at a Glance: 1st and 2nd Place

2004: Conservative over Liberal by 14,276 votes, 40% of votes cast.
2006: Conservative over Liberal by 21,356 votes, 54% of votes cast.
2008: Conservative over NDP by 17,543 votes, 55% of votes cast.
2011: Conservative over NDP by 18,478 votes, 53% of votes cast.
2015: Conservative over Liberal by 4,932 votes, 12% of votes cast.

Analysis

This riding typically votes Conservative. Voter turnout rose from 46% in 2011 to 54% in 2015.

Conservative MP Deepak Obhrai passed away in August. He was the Conservative Party's longest-serving MP.

Calgary Heritage, Electoral District #48007

Recommended Vote to Keep Your Guns

Vote for Conservative incumbent Bob Benzen.

History at a Glance: 1st and 2nd Place

2004: Conservative over Liberal by 25,796 votes, 50% of votes cast.
2006: Conservative over Liberal by 34,996 votes, 61% of votes cast.
2008: Conservative over Liberal by 33,630 votes, 64% of votes cast.
2011: Conservative over NDP by 36,175 votes, 63% of votes cast.
2015: Conservative over Liberal by 22,091 votes, 38% of votes cast.
2017 By-Election: Conservative over Liberal by 13,494 votes, 50% of votes cast.

Analysis

Former Conservative Prime Minister Stephen Harper's riding typically votes Conservative.

Voter turnout rose from 60% in 2011 to 72% in 2015.

Calgary Midnapore, Electoral District #48008

Recommended Vote to Keep Your Guns

Vote for Conservative incumbent Stephanie Kusie.

History at a Glance: 1st and 2nd Place

2004: Conservative over Liberal by 28,355 votes, 55% of votes cast.
2006: Conservative over Liberal by 38,794 votes, 65% of votes cast.
2008: Conservative over Green by 35,689 votes, 64% of votes cast.
2011: Conservative over NDP by 41,691 votes, 66% of votes cast.
2015: Conservative over Liberal by 28,019 votes, 44% of votes cast.
2017 By-Election: Conservative over Liberal by 17,504 votes, 60% of votes cast.

Analysis

Voter turnout rose from 59% in 2011 to 72% in 2015.

Calgary Nose Hill, Electoral District #48009

Recommended Vote to Keep Your Guns

Vote for Conservative incumbent Michelle Rempel.

History at a Glance: 1st and 2nd Place

2004: Conservative over Liberal by 20,037 votes, 41% of votes cast.
2006: Conservative over Liberal by 28,372 votes, 51% of votes cast.
2008: Conservative over Liberal by 28,372 votes, 56% of votes cast.
2011: Conservative over NDP by 33,195 votes, 58% of votes cast.
2015: Conservative over Liberal by 18,089 votes, 33% of votes cast.

Analysis

Voter turnout rose from 56% in 2011 to 66% in 2015. This riding typically votes Conservative and their candidates won the past five elections.

Calgary Rocky Ridge, Electoral District #48010

Recommended Vote to Keep Your Guns

Vote for Conservative incumbent Pat Kelly.

History at a Glance: 1st and 2nd Place

2015: Conservative over Liberal by 18,191 votes, 29% of votes cast.

Analysis

Conservative Pat Kelly won the first election after this riding was created.

Calgary Shepard, Electoral District #48011

Recommended Vote to Keep Your Guns

Vote for Conservative incumbent Tom Kmiec.

History at a Glance: 1st and 2nd Place

2015: Conservative over Liberal by 27,327 votes, 41% of votes cast.

Analysis

Conservative Tom Kmiec won the first election after this riding was created.

Calgary Signal Hill, Electoral District #48012

Recommended Vote to Keep Your Guns

Vote for Conservative incumbent Ron Liepert.

History at a Glance: 1st and 2nd Place

2004: Conservative over Liberal by 14,920 votes, 27% of votes cast.
2006: Conservative over Liberal by 23,692 votes, 37% of votes cast.
2008: Conservative over Liberal by 21,375 votes, 35% of votes cast.
2011: Conservative over Liberal by 28,622 votes, 44% of votes cast.
2015: Conservative over Liberal by 18,750 votes, 30% of votes cast.

Analysis

Voter turnout rose from 62% in 2011 to 73% in 2015. This riding typically votes Conservative. Their candidates won the past five elections.

Calgary Skyview, Electoral District #48013

Recommended Vote to Keep Your Guns

Vote Conservative.

History at a Glance: 1st and 2nd Place

2004: Conservative over Liberal by 13,252 votes, 38% of votes cast.
2006: Conservative over Liberal by 17,928 votes, 43% of votes cast.
2008: Conservative over Liberal by 11,484 votes, 31% of votes cast.
2011: Conservative over Liberal by 12,063 votes, 29% of votes cast.
2015: Liberal over Conservative by 2,759 votes, 6.1% of votes cast.

Analysis

Voter turnout rose from 47% in 2011 to 61% in 2015. This riding typically votes Conservative.

Edmonton Centre, Electoral District #48014

Recommended Vote to Keep Your Guns

Vote Conservative.

History at a Glance: 1st and 2nd Place

2004: Liberal over Conservative by 721 votes, 1.3% of votes cast.
2006: Conservative over Liberal by 3,609 votes, 6.3% of votes cast.
2008: Conservative over Liberal by 9,973 votes, 22% of votes cast.
2011: Conservative over NDP by 11,145 votes, 23% of votes cast.
2015: Liberal over Conservative by 1,199 votes, 2.2% of votes cast.

Analysis

Voter turnout rose from 57% in 2011 to 67% in 2015.

Edmonton Griesbach, Electoral District #48015

Recommended Vote to Keep Your Guns

Vote for Conservative incumbent Kerry Diotte.

History at a Glance: 1st and 2nd Place

2004: Conservative over Liberal by 5,974 votes, 14% of votes cast.
2006: Conservative over Liberal by 11,998 votes, 24% of votes cast.
2008: Conservative over NDP by 8,169 votes, 20% of votes cast.
2011: Conservative over NDP by 7,033 votes, 15% of votes cast.
2015: Conservative over NDP by 2,848 votes, 5.8% of votes cast.

Analysis

Voter turnout rose from 49% in 2011 to 60% in 2015. This riding typi-cally votes Conservative. Their candidates won the past five elections.

Edmonton Manning, Electoral District #48016

Recommended Vote to Keep Your Guns

Vote for Conservative incumbent Ziad Aboultaif.

History at a Glance: 1st and 2nd Place

2015: Conservative over Liberal by 8,657 votes, 18% of votes cast.

Analysis

This is electoral district was created in 2013 and Conservative candidate Ziad Aboultaif won in 2015.

Edmonton Mill Woods, Electoral District #48017

Recommended Vote to Keep Your Guns

Vote Conservative.

History at a Glance: 1st and 2nd Place

2015: Liberal over Conservative by 92 votes, 0.1% of votes cast.

Analysis

This electoral district was created in prior to Election 2015.

Edmonton Riverbend, Electoral District #48018

Recommended Vote to Keep Your Guns

Vote for Conservative incumbent Matt Jeneroux.

History at a Glance: 1st and 2nd Place

2004: Conservative over Liberal by 12,522 votes, 26% of votes cast.
2006: Conservative over Liberal by 22,908 votes, 41% of votes cast.
2008: Conservative over Liberal by 23,940 votes, 46% of votes cast.
2011: Conservative over NDP by 26,290 votes, 44% of votes cast.
2015: Conservative over Liberal by 11,377 votes, 20% of votes cast.

Analysis

Voter turnout rose from 59% in 2011 to 70% in 2015. This riding typically votes Conservative. Their candidates won the past five elections.

Edmonton Strathcona, Electoral District #48019

Recommended Vote to Keep Your Guns

Vote Conservative.

History at a Glance: 1st and 2nd Place

2004: Conservative over Liberal by 5,032 votes, 10% of votes cast.
2006: Conservative over NDP by 4,856 votes, 9.2% of votes cast.
2008: NDP over Conservative by 463 votes, 1.0% of votes cast.
2011: NDP over Conservative by 6,331 votes, 13% of votes cast.
2015: NDP over Conservative by 7,051 votes, 13% of votes cast.

Analysis

Voter turnout rose from 66% in 2011 to 70% in 2015. The NDP has defeated the Conservative candidates in this riding in each of the past three federal elections.

Edmonton West, Electoral District #48020

Recommended Vote to Keep Your Guns

Vote for Conservative incumbent Kelly McCauley.

History at a Glance: 1st and 2nd Place

2015: Conservative over Liberal by 7,721 votes, 14% of votes cast.

Analysis

Conservative Kelly McCauley won the first election after this riding was created.

Edmonton–Wetaskiwin, Electoral District #48021

Recommended Vote to Keep Your Guns

Vote for Conservative incumbent Mike Lake.

History at a Glance: 1st and 2nd Place

2004: Liberal over Conservative by 134 votes, 0.3% of votes cast.
2006: Conservative over Liberal by 17,382 votes, 37% of votes cast.
2008: Conservative over Liberal by 17,421 votes, 42% of votes cast.
2011: Conservative over NDP by 16,982 votes, 37% of votes cast.
2015: Conservative over Liberal by 30,289 votes, 44% of votes cast.

Analysis

Voter turnout rose from 53% in 2011 to 68% in 2015. This riding typically votes Conservative.

Foothills, Electoral District #48022

Recommended Vote to Keep Your Guns

Vote for Conservative incumbent John Barlow.

History at a Glance: 1st and 2nd Place

2004: Conservative over Liberal by 27,018 votes, 63% of votes cast.
2006: Conservative over Liberal by 32,938 votes, 66% of votes cast.
2008: Conservative over Green by 31,167 votes, 68% of votes cast.
2011: Conservative over NDP by 34,672 votes, 67% of votes cast.
2014 By-Election: Conservative over Liberal by 9,524 votes, or 52% of votes cast.
2015: Conservative over Liberal by 38,017 votes, 62% of votes cast.

Analysis

Voter turnout rose from 60% in 2011 to 73% in 2015. This riding typically votes Conservative. Their candidates won the past six elections, including the 2014 By-Election.

Fort McMurray–Cold Lake, Electoral District #48023

Recommended Vote to Keep Your Guns

Vote for Conservative incumbent David Yurdiga.

History at a Glance: 1st and 2nd Place

2004: Conservative over Liberal by 10,784 votes, 36% of votes cast.
2006: Conservative over Liberal by 15,737 votes, 50% of votes cast.
2008: Conservative over NDP by 13,860 votes, 54% of votes cast.
2011: Conservative over NDP by 17,935 votes, 59% of votes cast.
2014 By-Election: Conservative over Liberal by 1,462 votes, 11% of votes.
2015: Conservative over Liberal by 15,222 votes, 32% of votes cast.

Analysis

Voter turnout soared from 40% in 2011 to 61 in 2015, a huge jump since the last election. This riding typically votes Conservative and they've won the past six elections, including the 2014 By-Election.

Grande Prairie–Mackenzie, Electoral District #48024

Recommended Vote to Keep Your Guns

Vote for Conservative incumbent Chris Warkentin.

History at a Glance: 1st and 2nd Place

2004: Conservative over Liberal by 19,958 votes, 46% of votes cast.
2006: Conservative over Independent by 17,903 votes, 37% of votes cast.
2008: Conservative over NDP by 23,426 votes, 55% of votes cast.
2011: Conservative over Green by 28,594 votes, 60% of votes cast.
2015: Conservative over Liberal by 31,076 votes, 58% of votes cast.

Analysis

Voter turnout soared from 49% in 2011 to 65% in 2015, a huge jump since the last election. This riding typically votes Conservative. Their candidates won the past five elections.

Lakeland, Electoral District #48025

Recommended Vote to Keep Your Guns

Vote for Conservative incumbent Shannon Stubbs.

History at a Glance: 1st and 2nd Place

2015: Conservative over Liberal by 32,382 votes, 59% of votes cast.

Analysis

Lakeland, an amalgamation of two former electoral districts, is an area where voters overwhelmingly support the Conservative Party. Voter turnout rose from 55% in 2011 to 69% in 2015 and the margin of victory increased for the Conservative candidate.

Lethbridge, Electoral District #48026

Recommended Vote to Keep Your Guns

Vote for Conservative incumbent Rachael Harder.

History at a Glance: 1st and 2nd Place

2004: Conservative over Liberal by 19,515 votes, 41% of votes cast.
2006: Conservative over NDP by 27,926 votes, 54% of votes cast.
2008: Conservative over NDP by 24,981 votes, 53% of votes cast.
2011: Conservative over NDP by 14,101 votes, 29% of votes cast.
2015: Conservative over NDP by 20,647 votes, 36% of votes cast.

Analysis

Voter turnout rose from 53% in 2011 to 68% in 2015. This riding typically votes Conservative. Their candidates won the past five elections.

Medicine Hat–Cardston–Warner, Electoral District #48027

Recommended Vote to Keep Your Guns

Vote for Conservative incumbent Jim Hillyer.

History at a Glance: 1st and 2nd Place

2004: Conservative over Liberal by 25,910 votes, 65% of votes cast.
2006: Conservative over Liberal by 31,933 votes, 71% of votes cast.
2008: Conservative over NDP by 22,763 votes, 60% of votes cast.
2011: Conservative over NDP by 25,103 votes, 58% of votes cast.
2015: Conservative over Liberal by 25,764 votes, 51% of votes cast.
2016 By-Election: Conservative over Liberal by 15,155 votes, or 44% of votes cast.

Analysis

Voter turnout rose from 52% in 2011 to 65% in 2015. This riding typically votes Conservative. Their candidates won the past six elections.

Peace River–Westlock, Electoral District #48028

Recommended Vote to Keep Your Guns

Vote for Conservative incumbent Arnold Viersen.

History at a Glance: 1st and 2nd Place

2015: Conservative over NDP by 27,215 votes, 55% of votes cast.

Analysis

This electoral district was created prior to the 2015 federal election.

Red Deer–Mountain View, Electoral District #48029

Recommended Vote to Keep Your Guns

Vote for Conservative incumbent Earl Dreeshen.

History at a Glance: 1st and 2nd Place

2004: Conservative over Liberal by 28,216 votes, 63% of votes cast.
2006: Conservative over NDP by 33,341 votes, 66% of votes cast.
2008: Conservative over NDP by 28,186 votes, 62% of votes cast.
2011: Conservative over NDP by 30,393 votes, 61% of votes cast.
2015: Conservative over Liberal by 37,889 votes, 61% of votes cast.

Analysis

Voter turnout soared from 53% in 2011 to 70% in 2015. This riding typically votes Conservative. Their candidates won the past five elections.

Red Deer–Lacombe, Electoral District #48030

Recommended Vote to Keep Your Guns

Vote for Conservative incumbent Blaine Calkins.

History at a Glance: 1st and 2nd Place

2004: Conservative over Liberal by 26,316 votes, 62% of votes cast.
2006: Conservative over NDP by 31,335 votes, 66% of votes cast.
2008: Conservative over NDP by 28,892 votes, 69% of votes cast.
2011: Conservative over NDP by 32,475 votes, 70% of votes cast.
2015: Conservative over Liberal by 34,364 votes, 56% of votes cast.

Analysis

Voter turnout rose from 58% in 2011 to 69% in 2015. This riding typically votes Conservative. Their candidates won the past five elections.

St. Albert–Edmonton, Electoral District #48031

Recommended Vote to Keep Your Guns

Vote for Conservative incumbent Michael Cooper.

History at a Glance: 1st and 2nd Place

2004: Conservative over Liberal by 17,149 votes, 34% of votes cast.
2006: Conservative over Liberal by 23,104 votes, 39% of votes cast.
2008: Conservative over NDP by 23,391 votes, 46% of votes cast.
2011: Conservative over NDP by 22,824 votes, 42% of votes cast.
2015: Conservative over Liberal by 13,440 votes, 23% of votes cast.

Analysis

Voter turnout rose from 56% in 2011 to 70% in 2015. This riding typically votes Conservative. Their candidates won the past five elections.

Sherwood Park–Fort Saskatchewan, Electoral District #48032

Recommended Vote to Keep Your Guns

Vote for Conservative incumbent Garnett Genuis.

History at a Glance: 1st and 2nd Place

2004: Conservative over Liberal by 15,703 votes, 33% of votes cast.
2006: Conservative over Liberal by 26,939 votes, 50% of votes cast.
2008: Conservative over Independent by 1,668 votes, 3.4% of votes cast.
2011: Conservative over Independent by 8,360 votes, 15% of votes cast.
2015: Conservative over Liberal by 29,027 votes, 44% of votes cast.

Analysis

Voter turnout soared from 58% in 2011 to 74% in 2015. This riding typically votes Conservative and their candidates won the past five elections.

Sturgeon River–Parkland, Electoral District #48033

Recommended Vote to Keep Your Guns

Vote for Conservative incumbent Dane Lloyd.

History at a Glance: 1st and 2nd Place

2004: Conservative over Liberal by 17,585 votes, 35% of votes cast.
2006: Conservative over Liberal by 29,050 votes, 50% of votes cast.
2008: Conservative over NDP by 29,775 votes, 56% of votes cast.
2011: Conservative over NDP by 32,510 votes, 55% of votes cast.
2015: Conservative over Liberal by 33,634 votes, 55% of votes cast.

Analysis

Voter turnout soared from 56% in 2011 to 71% in 2015. This riding was created in 2004 and Conservative Rona Ambrose won it from then until the 2015 election. When she retired, Conservative Dane Lloyd carried on the tradition of winning by a huge margin.

Yellowhead, Electoral District #48034

Recommended Vote to Keep Your Guns

Vote Conservative.

History at a Glance: 1st and 2nd Place

2004: Conservative over Liberal by 22,062 votes, 57% of votes cast.
2006: Conservative over NDP by 25,928 votes, 60% of votes cast.
2008: Conservative over NDP by 22,276 votes, 60% of votes cast.
2011: Conservative over NDP by 26,514 votes, 64% of votes cast.
2014 By-Election: Conservative over Liberal by 2,369 votes, or 19% of votes cast.
2015: Conservative over Liberal by 30,483 votes, 58% of votes cast.

Analysis

Voter turnout rose from 55% in 2011 to 69% in 2015. This riding typically votes Conservative. Their candidates won the past six elections, including the 2014 By-Election where Jim Eglinski took over for Rob Merrifield.

Eglinski will retire before the 2019 federal election.

British Columbia

Abbotsford, Electoral District #59001

Recommended Vote to Keep Your Guns

Vote for Conservative incumbent Ed Fast.

History at a Glance: 1st and 2nd Place

2004: Conservative over Liberal by 19,970 votes, 41% of votes cast.
2006: Conservative over NDP by 21,821 votes, 46% of votes cast.
2008: Conservative over Liberal by 22,920 votes, 47% of votes cast.
2011: Conservative over NDP by 22,404 votes, 45% of votes cast.
2015: Conservative over Liberal by 7,452 votes, 15% of votes cast.

Analysis

This riding tends to vote Conservative. Their candidates won the past five elections and voter turnout rose from 59% in 2011 to 69% in 2015.

Burnaby North–Seymour, Electoral District #59002

Recommended Vote to Keep Your Guns

Vote Conservative.

History at a Glance: 1st and 2nd Place

2004: NDP over Liberal by 934 votes, 2.1% of votes cast.
2006: NDP over Liberal by 1,244 votes, 2.6% of votes cast.
2008: NDP over Conservative by 798 votes, 1.7% of votes cast.
2011: NDP over Conservative by 1,011 votes, 2.1% of votes cast.
2015: Liberal over NDP by 3,401 votes, 6.4% of votes cast.

Analysis

Election 2015 was the first win for the Liberals in the past five elections. This riding tends to vote NDP, but, in both 2008 and 2011 the Conservative candidate lost by a tiny margin. Voter turnout rose from 57% in 2011 to 70% in 2015.

Burnaby South, Electoral District #59003

Recommended Vote to Keep Your Guns

Vote for NDP incumbent Jagmeet Singh.

History at a Glance: 1st and 2nd Place 1st

2015: NDP over Liberal by 547 votes, or 1.2% of votes cast.
2019 By-Election: NDP over Liberal by 2,929 votes, or 13% of votes cast.

Analysis

This electoral district was created prior to the 2015 federal election. NDP Leader Jagmeet Singh won the 2019 by-election and is favoured to win the general election.

Cariboo–Prince George, Electoral District #59004

Recommended Vote to Keep Your Guns

Vote for Conservative incumbent Todd Doherty.

History at a Glance: 1st and 2nd Place

2004: Conservative over Independent by 8,538 votes, 16% of votes cast.
2006: Conservative over Liberal by 9,115 votes, 17% of votes cast.
2008: Conservative over NDP by 12,056 votes, 29% of votes cast.
2011: Conservative over NDP by 11,308 votes, 26% of votes cast.
2015: Conservative over Liberal by 2,767 votes, 5.1% of votes cast.

Analysis

This riding tends to vote Conservative. Their candidates won the past five elections and voter turnout rose from 57% in 2011 to 68% in 2015.

Central Okanagan–Similkameen–Nicola, Electoral District #59005

Recommended Vote to Keep Your Guns

Vote for Conservative incumbent Dan Albas.

History at a Glance: 1st and 2nd Place

2004: Conservative over Liberal by 13,008 votes, 27% of votes cast.
2006: Conservative over Liberal by 13,703 votes, 27% of votes cast.
2008: Conservative over NDP by 20,529 votes, 41% of votes cast.
2011: Conservative over NDP by 15,672 votes, 29% of votes cast.
2015: Conservative over Liberal by 1,458 votes, 2.4% of votes cast.

Analysis

This riding tends to vote Conservative. Their candidates won the past five elections. Voter turnout rose from 62% in 2011 to 71% in 2015.

Chilliwack–Hope, Electoral District #59006

Recommended Vote to Keep Your Guns

Vote for Conservative incumbent Mark Strahl.

History at a Glance: 1st and 2nd Place

2004: Conservative over NDP by 14,852 votes, 33% of votes cast.
2006: Conservative over NDP by 16,827 votes, 35% of votes cast.
2008: Conservative over NDP by 20,407 votes, 44% of votes cast.
2011: Conservative over NDP by 15,469 votes, 31% of votes cast.
2015: Conservative over Liberal by 4,331 votes, 8.5% of votes cast.

Analysis

This riding tends to vote Conservative. Their candidates won the past five elections. Voter turnout rose from 58% in 2011 to 70% in 2015.

Cloverdale–Langley City, Electoral District #59007

Recommended Vote to Keep Your Guns

Vote Conservative.

History at a Glance: 1st and 2nd Place

2015: Liberal over Conservative by 5,817 votes, 11% of votes cast.

Analysis

This electoral district was created prior to the 2015 federal election. Voters in this area typically support Conservative candidates.

Conservative Mark Warawa won the riding of Langley in five elections.

Coquitlam–Port Coquitlam, Electoral District #59008

Recommended Vote to Keep Your Guns

Vote Conservative.

History at a Glance: 1st and 2nd Place

2004: Conservative over Liberal by 6,219 votes, 14% of votes cast.
2006: Conservative over Liberal by 6,827 votes, 14% of votes cast.
2008: Conservative over NDP by 15,117 votes, 32% of votes cast.
2011: Conservative over NDP by 12,581 votes, 26% of votes cast.
2015: Liberal over Conservative by 1,855 votes, 3.3% of votes cast.

Analysis

This riding tends to vote Conservative. Their candidates won four of the past five elections. Voter turnout rose from 56% in 2011 to 66% in 2015.

Courtenay–Alberni, Electoral District #59009

Recommended Vote to Keep Your Guns

Vote Conservative.

History at a Glance: 1st and 2nd Place

2004: Conservative over NDP by 4,006 votes, 6.8% of votes cast.
2006: Conservative over NDP by 5,767 votes, 8.7% of votes cast.
2008: Conservative over NDP by 9,250 votes, 15% of votes cast.
2011: Conservative over NDP by 5,304 votes, 8.1% of votes cast.
2015: NDP over Conservative by 6,868 votes, 9.8% of votes cast.

Analysis

This riding tends to vote Conservative. Their candidates won four of the past five elections. Voter turnout rose from 67% in 2011 to 76% in 2015.

Cowichan–Malahat–Langford, Electoral District #59010

Recommended Vote to Keep Your Guns

Vote Conservative.

History at a Glance: 1st and 2nd Place

2004: NDP over Conservative by 6,315 votes, 11% of votes cast.
2006: NDP over Conservative by 8,943 votes, 15% of votes cast.
2008: NDP over Conservative by 4,610 votes, 7.6% of votes cast.
2011: NDP over Conservative by 6,775 votes, 11% of votes cast.
2015: NDP over Liberal by 7,515 votes, 12% of votes cast.

Analysis

Projections in late August show a tight three-way race between the Conservatives, NDP and Greens, which could potentially end the NDP's dominance in this riding.

Voter turnout rose from 64% in 2011 to 75% in 2015.

Delta, Electoral District #59011

Recommended Vote to Keep Your Guns

Vote Conservative.

History at a Glance: 1st and 2nd Place

2015: Liberal over Conservative by 9,100 votes, 16% of votes cast.

Analysis

This electoral district was created prior to the 2015 federal election but voters in this area typically support Conservative candidates.

Esquimalt–Saanich–Sooke, Electoral District #59026

Recommended Vote to Keep Your Guns

Vote Conservative.

History at a Glance: 1st and 2nd Place

2004: Liberal over NDP by 2,568 votes, 4.7% of votes cast.
2006: Liberal over NDP by 2,166 votes, 3.6% of votes cast.
2008: Liberal over Conservative by 68 votes, 0.1% of votes cast.
2011: NDP over Conservative by 406 votes, 0.6% of votes cast.
2015: NDP over Liberal by 5,214 votes, 7.7% of votes cast.

Analysis

The NDP won the past two elections, ending a Liberal streak in this riding. Voter turnout rose from 65% in 2011 to 75% in 2015.

Fleetwood–Port Kells, Electoral District #59012

Recommended Vote to Keep Your Guns

Vote Conservative.

History at a Glance: 1st and 2nd Place

2004: Conservative over Liberal by 2,484 votes, 6.3% of votes cast.
2006: Conservative over Liberal by 828 votes, 1.9% of votes cast.
2008: Conservative over Liberal by 8,887 votes, 19% of votes cast.
2011: Conservative over NDP by 7,417 votes, 15% of votes cast.
2015: Liberal over Conservative by 8,596 votes, 18% of votes cast.

Analysis

This riding tends to vote Conservative. Their candidates won four of the past five elections. Voter turnout rose from 53% in 2011 to 65% in 2015.

Kamloops–Thompson–Cariboo, Electoral District #59013

Recommended Vote to Keep Your Guns

Vote for Conservative incumbent Cathy McLeod.

History at a Glance: 1st and 2nd Place

2004: Conservative over Liberal by 6,177 votes, 12% of votes cast.
2006: Conservative over NDP by 4,531 votes, 8.5% of votes cast.
2008: Conservative over NDP by 5,608 votes, 10% of votes cast.
2011: Conservative over NDP by 8,699 votes, 15% of votes cast.
2015: Conservative over NDP by 3,129 votes, 4.5% of votes cast.

Analysis

This riding tends to vote Conservative. Their candidates won the past five elections. Voter turnout rose from 63% in 2011 to 73% in 2015.

Kelowna–Lake Country, Electoral District #59014

Recommended Vote to Keep Your Guns

Vote Conservative.

History at a Glance: 1st and 2nd Place

2004: Conservative over Liberal by 11,444 votes, 21% of votes cast.
2006: Conservative over Liberal by 13,367 votes, 23% of votes cast.
2008: Conservative over NDP by 23,283 votes, 41% of votes cast.
2011: Conservative over NDP by 21,244 votes, 35% of votes cast.
2015: Liberal over Conservative by 4,112 votes, 6.4% of votes cast.

Analysis

This riding tends to vote Conservative. Their candidates won four of the past five elections. Voter turnout rose from 60% in 2011 to 70% in 2015.

Kootenay–Columbia, Electoral District #59015

Recommended Vote to Keep Your Guns

Vote Conservative.

History at a Glance: 1st and 2nd Place

2004: Conservative over NDP by 11,564 votes, 28% of votes cast.
2006: Conservative over NDP by 11,621 votes, 28% of votes cast.
2008: Conservative over NDP by 14,510 votes, 37% of votes cast.
2011: Conservative over NDP by 9,711 votes, 23% of votes cast.
2015: NDP over Conservative by 282 votes, 0.4% of votes cast.

Analysis

This riding tends to vote Conservative. Their candidates won four of the past five elections. Voter turnout rose from 63% in 2011 to 73% in 2015.

Langley–Aldergrove, Electoral District #59016

Recommended Vote to Keep Your Guns

Vote Conservative.

History at a Glance: 1st and 2nd Place

2004: Conservative over Liberal by 11,741 votes, 23% of votes cast.
2006: Conservative over Liberal by 16,024 votes, 29% of votes cast.
2008: Conservative over NDP by 23,640 votes, 45% of votes cast.
2011: Conservative over NDP by 24,214 votes, 44% of votes cast.
2015: Conservative over Liberal by 5,278 votes, 8.9% of votes cast.

Analysis

This riding tends to vote Conservative and their candidates won the past five elections. Voter turnout rose from 61% in 2011 to 71% in 2015.

Mission–Matsqui–Fraser Canyon, Electoral District #59017

Recommended Vote to Keep Your Guns

Vote for Conservative candidate Brad Vis.

History at a Glance: 1st and 2nd Place

2015: Liberal over Conservative by 1,038 votes, 2.3% of votes cast.

Analysis

This electoral district was created prior to the 2015 federal election and voters in this area typically support Conservative candidates.

Nanaimo–Ladysmith, Electoral District #59018

Recommended Vote to Keep Your Guns

Vote Conservative.

History at a Glance: 1st and 2nd Place

2015: NDP over Liberal by 6,898 votes, 9.7% of votes cast.
2019 By-Election: Green over Conservative by 5,087 votes, 12% of votes.

Analysis

This electoral district was created prior to the 2015 federal election and voters in this area typically support NDP candidates.

New Westminster–Burnaby, Electoral District #59019

Recommended Vote to Keep Your Guns

Vote for NDP incumbent Peter Julian.

History at a Glance: 1st and 2nd Place

2004: NDP over Liberal by 329 votes, 0.8% of votes cast.
2006: NDP over Liberal by 3,971 votes, 8.9% of votes cast.
2008: NDP over Conservative by 6,995 votes, 16% of votes cast.
2011: NDP over Conservative by 6,184 votes, 14% of votes cast.
2015: NDP over Liberal by 7,623 votes, 14% of votes cast.

Analysis

This riding tends to vote NDP. Their candidates won the past five elections. Voter turnout rose from 53% in 2011 to 65% in 2015.

North Island–Powell River, Electoral District #59037

Recommended Vote to Keep Your Guns

Vote Conservative.

History at a Glance: 1st and 2nd Place

2004: Conservative over NDP by 483 votes, 0.9% of votes cast.
2006: NDP over Conservative by 616 votes, 1.1% of votes cast.
2008: Conservative over NDP by 2,497 votes, 4.4% of votes cast.
2011: Conservative over NDP by 1,827 votes, 3.1% of votes cast.
2015: NDP over Conservative by 8,500 votes, 14% of votes cast.

Analysis

This riding tends to vote Conservative. Their candidates won three of the past five elections. Voter turnout rose from 65% in 2011 to 74% in 2015.

North Okanagan–Shuswap, Electoral District #59020

Recommended Vote to Keep Your Guns

Vote for Conservative incumbent Mel Arnold.

History at a Glance: 1st and 2nd Place

2004: Conservative over NDP by 11,486 votes, 15% of votes cast.
2006: Conservative over NDP by 9,897 votes, 18% of votes cast.
2008: Conservative over NDP by 17,338 votes, 32% of votes cast.
2011: Conservative over NDP by 16,484 votes, 29% of votes cast.
2015: Conservative over Liberal by 6,541 votes, 9.4% of votes cast.

Analysis

This riding tends to vote Conservative. Their candidates won the past five elections. Voter turnout rose from 62% in 2011 to 72% in 2015.

North Vancouver, Electoral District #59021

Recommended Vote to Keep Your Guns

Vote Conservative

History at a Glance: 1st and 2nd Place

2004: Liberal over Conservative by 2,071 votes, 3.7% of votes cast.
2006: Liberal over Conservative by 3,336 votes, 5.6% of votes cast.
2008: Conservative over Liberal by 2,820 votes, 4.9% of votes cast.
2011: Conservative over Liberal by 11,331 votes, 19% of votes cast.
2015: Liberal over Conservative by 19,157 votes, 30% of votes cast.

Analysis

This riding tends to bounce between Liberal and Conservative candidates by narrow margins. Voter turnout rose from 67% in 2011 to 76% in 2015.

Pitt Meadows–Maple Ridge, Electoral District #59022

Recommended Vote to Keep Your Guns

Vote Conservative.

History at a Glance: 1st and 2nd Place

2004: Conservative over NDP by 2,797 votes, 5.8% of votes cast.
2006: Conservative over NDP by 2,721 votes, 5.2% of votes cast.
2008: Conservative over NDP by 9,618 votes, 19% of votes cast.
2011: Conservative over NDP by 9,968 votes, 19% of votes cast.
2015: Liberal over Conservative by 1,300 votes, 2.5% of votes cast.

Analysis

This riding tends to vote Conservative. Election 2015 was the first win for the Liberals in the past five elections. Voter turnout rose from 59% in 2011 to 72% in 2015.

Port Moody–Coquitlam, Electoral District #59023

Recommended Vote to Keep Your Guns

Vote Conservative.

History at a Glance: 1st and 2nd Place

2004: Conservative over NDP by 113 votes, 0.2% of votes cast.
2006: NDP over Conservative by 2,933 votes, 5.8% of votes cast.
2008: NDP over Conservative by 1,488 votes, 3.0% of votes cast.
2011: NDP over Conservative by 2,247 votes, 4.5% of votes cast.
2015: NDP over Liberal by 2,818 votes, 5.2% of votes cast.

Analysis

This riding tends to vote NDP. Their candidates won four of the past five elections, including Election 2015. The NDP incumbent will not run again in 2019.

Voter turnout rose from 59% in 2011 to 69% in 2015.

Prince George–Peace River–Northern Rockies, Electoral District #59024

Recommended Vote to Keep Your Guns

Vote for Conservative incumbent Bob Zimmer.

History at a Glance: 1st and 2nd Place

2004: Conservative over NDP by 13,780 votes, 38% of votes cast.
2006: Conservative over NDP by 16,035 votes, 43% of votes cast.
2008: Conservative over NDP by 16,155 votes, 46% of votes cast.
2011: Conservative over NDP by 14,070 votes, 37% of votes cast.
2015: Conservative over Liberal by 14,324 votes, 28% of votes cast.

Analysis

This riding tends to vote Conservative. Their candidates won the past five elections. Voter turnout rose from 53% in 2011 to 66% in 2015.

Richmond Centre, Electoral District #59025

Recommended Vote to Keep Your Guns

Vote for Conservative incumbent Alice Wong.

History at a Glance: 1st and 2nd Place

2004: Liberal over Conservative by 3,747 votes, 9.2% of votes cast.
2006: Liberal over Conservative by 1,808 votes, 4.1% of votes cast.
2008: Conservative over Liberal by 8,138 votes, 19% of votes cast.
2011: Conservative over Liberal by 17,082 votes, 40% of votes cast.
2015: Conservative over Liberal by 1,136 votes, 2.8% of votes cast.

Analysis

This riding tends to vote Conservative. Their candidates won three of the past five elections, including Election 2015. Voter turnout rose from 50% in 2011 to 57% in 2015.

Saanich–Gulf Islands, Electoral District #59027

Recommended Vote to Keep Your Guns

Vote Conservative.

History at a Glance: 1st and 2nd Place

2004: Conservative over Liberal by 4,968 votes, 7.8% of votes cast.
2006: Conservative over NDP by 6,971 votes, 11% of votes cast.
2008: Conservative over Liberal by 2,625 votes, 3.9% of votes cast.
2011: Green over Conservative by 7,346 votes, 11% of votes cast.
2015: Green over Conservative by 23,810 votes, 35% of votes cast.

Analysis

This riding tended to vote Conservative before handing it to the Green Party, who wants to ban guns.

Voter turnout rose from 74% in 2011 to 78% in 2015.

Skeena–Bulkley Valley, Electoral District #59028

Recommended Vote to Keep Your Guns

Vote Conservative.

History at a Glance: 1st and 2nd Place

2004: NDP over Conservative by 1,272 votes, 3.4% of votes cast.
2006: NDP over Conservative by 5,866 votes, 15% of votes cast.
2008: NDP over Conservative by 4,658 votes, 13% of votes cast.
2011: NDP over Conservative by 7,314 votes, 21% of votes cast.
2015: NDP over Conservative by 11,595 votes, 26% of votes cast.

Analysis

This riding tends to vote NDP. The NDP incumbent will not run again in 2019, opening the door for the Conservative Party.

Voter turnout rose from 58% in 2011 to 68% in 2015.

South Okanagan–West Kootenay, Electoral District #59029

Recommended Vote to Keep Your Guns

Vote Conservative.

History at a Glance: 1st and 2nd Place

2004: Conservative over NDP by 680 votes, 1.2% of votes cast.
2006: NDP over Liberal by 13,359 votes, 29% of votes cast.
2008: NDP over Conservative by 5,571 votes, 12% of votes cast.
2011: NDP over Conservative by 5,933 votes, 12% of votes cast.
2015: NDP over Conservative by 4,952 votes, 7.4% of votes cast.

Analysis

This riding tends to vote NDP. Their candidates won four of the past five elections, including Election 2015. They defeated the Conservative candidate in each of the past three elections. Voter turnout rose from 65% in 2011 to 72% in 2015.

South Surrey–White Rock, Electoral District #59030

Recommended Vote to Keep Your Guns

Vote Conservative.

History at a Glance: 1st and 2nd Place

2004: Conservative over Liberal by 3,149 votes, 5.9% of votes cast.
2006: Conservative over Liberal by 9,047 votes, 16% of votes cast.
2008: Conservative over Liberal by 19,701 votes, 36% of votes cast.
2011: Conservative over NDP by 20,109 votes, 41% of votes cast.
2015: Conservative over Liberal by 1,439 votes, 2.5% of votes cast.
2017 By-Election: Liberal over Conservative by 1,545 votes, 5.1% of votes cast.

Analysis

This riding tends to vote Conservative. Their candidates won the past five elections and narrowly lost the 2017 By-Election. Voter turnout soared from 54% in 2011 to 74% in 2015, but dropped by half during the 2017 by-election.

Steveston–Richmond East, Electoral District #59031

Recommended Vote to Keep Your Guns

Vote Conservative.

History at a Glance: 1st and 2nd Place

2004: Conservative over Liberal by 5,793 votes, 12% of votes cast.
2006: Conservative over Liberal by 8,068 votes, 17% of votes cast.
2008: Conservative over Liberal by 15,881 votes, 34% of votes cast.
2011: Conservative over NDP by 14,878 votes, 31% of votes cast.
2015: Liberal over Conservative by 2,856 votes, 6.6% of votes cast.

Analysis

This riding tends to vote Conservative. Their candidates won four of the past five elections. Election 2015 was the first win for the Liberals in the past five elections. Voter turnout remaining almost unchanged at 59% in 2011 and 60% in 2015.

Surrey Centre, Electoral District #59032

Recommended Vote to Keep Your Guns

Vote Conservative.

History at a Glance: 1st and 2nd Place

2004: Independent over NDP by 6,777 votes, 20% of votes cast.
2006: NDP over Conservative by 6,443 votes, 18% of votes cast.
2008: Conservative over NDP by 1,106 votes, 2.8% of votes cast.
2011: NDP over Conservative by 1,497 votes, 4.0% of votes cast.
2015: Liberal over NDP by 6,479 votes, 15% of votes cast.

Analysis

Election 2015 was the first win for the Liberals in the past five elections. Voter turnout rose from 51% in 2011 to 60% in 2015.

Surrey–Newton, Electoral District #59033

Recommended Vote to Keep Your Guns

Vote Conservative.

History at a Glance: 1st and 2nd Place

2004: Conservative over Liberal by 520 votes, 1.3% of votes cast.
2006: Liberal over NDP by 1,000 votes, 2.3% of votes cast.
2008: Liberal over Conservative by 2,493 votes, 5.5% of votes cast.
2011: NDP over Liberal by 903 votes, 2.0% of votes cast.
2015: Liberal over NDP by 13,267 votes, 30% of votes cast.

Analysis

This riding tends to vote Liberal. Their candidates won three of the past five elections, including Election 2015. Voter turnout rose from 61% in 2011 to 67% in 2015.

Vancouver Centre, Electoral District #59034

Recommended Vote to Keep Your Guns

Vote Conservative

History at a Glance: 1st and 2nd Place

2004: Liberal over NDP by 4,230 votes, 6.1% of votes cast.
2006: Liberal over NDP by 8,639 votes, 15% of votes cast.
2008: Liberal over Conservative by 5,318 votes, 9.4% of votes cast.
2011: Liberal over NDP by 2,935 votes, 4.0% of votes cast.
2015: Liberal over NDP by 20,936 votes, 36% of votes cast.

Analysis

This riding tends to vote Liberal but the battle in four of the past five elections was between the Liberal and NDP candidates. In 2011 both the NDP (2,935 votes) and the Conservatives (2,937 votes) came within striking distance of winning.

Voter turnout dropped from 73% in 2011 to 66% in 2015.

Vancouver East, Electoral District #59035

Recommended Vote to Keep Your Guns

Vote for NDP incumbent Jenny Kwan.

History at a Glance: 1st and 2nd Place

2004: NDP over Liberal by 12,684 votes, 31% of votes cast.
2006: NDP over Liberal by 14,020 votes, 33% of votes cast.
2008: NDP over Liberal by 15,379 votes, 37% of votes cast.
2011: NDP over Conservative by 19,433 votes, 44% of votes cast.
2015: NDP over Liberal by 12,784 votes, 17% of votes cast.

Analysis

This riding tends to vote NDP. Their candidates won the past five elections. Voter turnout soared from 54% in 2011 to 84% in 2015, a huge jump since the last election.

Vancouver Granville, Electoral District #59036

Recommended Vote to Keep Your Guns

Vote for Independent Jody Wilson-Raybould as the best choice to defeat the Liberals.

History at a Glance: 1st and 2nd Place

2015: Liberal over NDP by 9,181 votes, 17% of votes cast.

Analysis

Wilson-Raybould was elected as a Liberal in 2015. The prime minister expelled her from the party in 2019.

This electoral district was created prior to the 2015 federal election.

Vancouver Kingsway, Electoral District #59038

Recommended Vote to Keep Your Guns

Vote for NDP incumbent Don Davies.

History at a Glance: 1st and 2nd Place

2004: Liberal over NDP by 1,351 votes, 2.3% of votes cast.
2006: Liberal over NDP by 4,592 votes, 8.4% of votes cast.
2008: NDP over Liberal by 2,769 votes, 6.1% of votes cast.
2011: NDP over Conservative by 10,295 votes, 22% of votes cast.
2015: NDP over Liberal by 8,138 votes, 18% of votes cast.

Analysis

The NDP won the past three elections. Voter turnout rose from 57% in 2011 to 63% in 2015.

Vancouver Quadra, Electoral District #59039

Recommended Vote to Keep Your Guns

Vote Conservative.

History at a Glance: 1st and 2nd Place

2004: Liberal over Conservative by 14,539 votes, 26% of votes cast.
2006: Liberal over Conservative by 11,811 votes, 20% of votes cast.
2008: Liberal over Conservative by 4,832 votes, 8.7% of votes cast.
2011: Liberal over Conservative by 1,919 votes, 3.5% of votes cast.
2015: Liberal over Conservative by 17,419 votes, 33% of votes cast.

Analysis

This riding tends to vote Liberal. Their candidates won the past five elections. Voter turnout rose from 62% in 2011 to 70% in 2015.

Vancouver South, Electoral District #59040

Recommended Vote to Keep Your Guns

Vote Conservative.

History at a Glance: 1st and 2nd Place

2004: Liberal over Conservative by 7,770 votes, 19% of votes cast.
2006: Liberal over Conservative by 9,135 votes, 21% of votes cast.
2008: Liberal over Conservative by 20 votes, 0.0% of votes cast.
2011: Conservative over Liberal by 3,900 votes, 8.7% of votes cast.
2015: Liberal over Conservative by 6,658 votes, 15% of votes cast.

Analysis

This riding tends to vote Liberal. Their candidates won four of the past five elections, including Election 2015. Voter turnout rose from 55% in 2011 to 63% in 2015.

Victoria, Electoral District #59041

Recommended Vote to Keep Your Guns

Vote NDP because they are your best choice to defeat the Liberals.

History at a Glance: 1st and 2nd Place

2004: Liberal over NDP by 2,305 votes, 4.0% of votes cast.
2006: NDP over Liberal by 6,783 votes, 11% of votes cast.
2008: NDP over Conservative by 10,106 votes, 17% of votes cast.
2011: NDP over Conservative by 16,404 votes, 27% of votes cast.
2012 By-Election: NDP over Green by 1,118 votes, or 5.8% of votes.
2015: NDP over Green by 6,731 votes, 9.4% of votes cast.

Analysis

The NDP won the past five elections, including the 2012 by-election. The NDP incumbent will not run again in 2019. Voter turnout rose from 67% in 2011 to 76% in 2015.

West Vancouver–Sunshine Coast–Sea to Sky Country, Electoral District #59042

Recommended Vote to Keep Your Guns

Vote Conservative.

History at a Glance: 1st and 2nd Place

2004: Conservative over Liberal by 1,687 votes, 2.8% of votes cast.
2006: Liberal over Conservative by 976 votes, 1.5% of votes cast.
2008: Conservative over Liberal by 10,880 votes, 18% of votes cast.
2011: Conservative over NDP by 13,786 votes, 36% of votes cast.
2015: Liberal over Conservative by 18,889 votes, 28% of votes cast.

Analysis

The Conservatives won three of the past five elections, and lost to the Liberals in 2015. Voter turnout rose from 39% in 2011 to 73% in 2015.

Yukon

Electoral District #60001 Yukon

Recommended Vote to Keep Your Guns

Vote Conservative.

History at a Glance: 1st and 2nd Place

2004: Liberal over NDP by 2,508 votes, 20% of votes cast.
2006: Liberal over NDP by 3,481 votes, 25% of votes cast.
2008: Liberal over Conservative by 1,927 votes, 13% of votes cast.
2011: Conservative over Liberal by 132 votes, 0.8% of votes cast.
2015: Liberal over Conservative by 5,959 votes, 29% of votes cast.

Analysis

This riding tends to vote Liberal. Their candidates won four of the past five elections, including Election 2015. Voter turnout rose from 66% in 2011 to 75% in 2015.

Northwest Territories

Electoral District #61001 Northwest Territories

Recommended Vote to Keep Your Guns

Vote NDP because they are your best choice to defeat the Liberals.

History at a Glance: 1st and 2nd Place

2004: Liberal over NDP by 53 votes, 0.4% of votes cast.
2006: NDP over Liberal by 1,159 votes, 7.2% of votes cast.
2008: NDP over Conservative by 523 votes, 3.8% of votes cast.
2011: NDP over Conservative by 2,139 votes, 14% of votes cast.
2015: Liberal over NDP by 3,389 votes, 18% of votes cast.

Analysis

Voter turnout rose from 54% in 2011 to 63% in 2015.

Nunavut

Nunavut, Electoral District #62001

Recommended Vote to Keep Your Guns

Vote Conservative.

History at a Glance: 1st and 2nd Place

2004: Liberal over Independent by 2,646 votes, 36% of votes cast.
2006: Liberal over Conservative by 1,003 votes, 11% of votes cast.
2008: Conservative over Liberal by 466 votes, 5.8% of votes cast.
2011: Conservative over Liberal by 1,670 votes, 21% of votes cast.
2015: Liberal over NDP by 2,448 votes, 21% of votes cast.

Analysis

Voter turnout rose from 45% in 2011 to 59% in 2015.

Facts and Stats

As of Spring 2019, Individuals

Total Licencees   2,186,161 (7% of Voters)
"Non-restricted" Licencees 1,600,000
"Restricted" Licencees   608,649
"Prohibited" Licencees   48,399
Owners of Handguns   260,677 (less than 1% of Voters)

Privately Owned Firearms Registered With the RCMP

Total   1.03 Million
Handguns   936,459
Rifles   93,188
AR-15 Target Rifles   68,000
Shotguns   324

Other

Firearm Businesses   1,500
Target Ranges   1,400

If you are a gun owner who isn't politically active today...

You won't be a gun owner tomorrow.

EndNotes

1 https://policyoptions.irpp.org/fr/magazines/march-2018/gun-control-still-a-key-issue-for-centre-left-voters/

2 https://medium.com/@kashani/there-is-actually-a-way-to-guarantee-harper-s-defeat-here-s-how-11ca79cec748

3 https://www.theglobeandmail.com/politics/article-liberals-want-to-prohibit-more-assault-weapons-rather-than-ban/

4 https://thegunblog.ca/2019/08/13/trudeau-says-election-plan-against-gun-owners-is-coming/

5 https://www.macleans.ca/politics/ottawa/the-rise-and-fall-of-justin-trudeaus-political-honeymoon/

6 https://www.cbc.ca/news/politics/grenier-conserva-tives-ndp-1.4912981

7 https://twitter.com/AKimCampbell/status/1126956694989344770

8 https://policyoptions.irpp.org/magazines/march-2018/gun-control-still-a-key-issue-for-centre-left-voters/

9 http://338canada.com

10 https://www.youtube.com/watch?v=lqnwdIGUAHs

11 http://338canada.com/districts/24007e.htm

12 https://twitter.com/JohnTory/status/1158467635413229574

13 Reasons Why Every Vote Counts

In Election 2015 the average electoral district had 81,000 eligible voters. In these 13 ridings the winner was decided by 500 or fewer ballots, or roughly one half of 1% of eligible votes. In one case, by one tenth of 1%.

In Election 2019, your vote counts. So do the votes of everyone in your personal sphere of influence (your family, friends, neighbours and co-workers).

1. **Elmwood–Transcona (MB):** NDP defeated Conservative by 61 votes, 0.14% of votes cast.

2. **Desnethé–Missinippi–Churchill River (MB):** NDP defeated Liberal by 82 votes, 0.27% of votes cast.

3. **Barrie–Springwater–Oro-Medonte (ON):** Conservative defeated Liberal by 86 votes, 0.17% of votes cast.

4. **Edmonton Mill Woods (AB):** Liberal defeated Conservative by 92 votes, 0.13% of votes cast.

5. **Regina–Lewvan (SK):** NDP defeated Conservative by 132 votes, 0.28% of votes cast.

6. **Pierre-Boucher–Les Patriotes–Verchères (QC):** Bloc Québécois defeated Liberal by 213 votes, 0.36% of votes cast.

7. **Hastings–Lennox and Addington (ON):** Liberal defeated Conservative by 225 votes, 0.45% of votes cast.

8. **Kitchener–Conestoga (ON):** Conservative defeated Liberal by 251 votes, 0.53% of votes cast.

9. **Montmagny–L'Islet–Kamouraska–Rivière-du-Loup (QC):** Conservative defeated Liberal by 272 votes, 0.55% of votes.

10. **Kootenay–Columbia (BC):** NDP defeated Conservative by 282 votes, 0.45% of votes cast.

11. **Jonquière (QC):** NDP defeated Liberal by 339 votes, 0.7% votes.

12. **Kenora (ON):** Liberal defeated NDP by 441 votes, 1.44% of votes cast.

13. **Hochelaga:** NDP defeated Liberal by 500 votes, 0.93% of votes cast.

www.ingramcontent.com/pod-product-compliance
Lightning Source LLC
Chambersburg PA
CBHW061007280326
41935CB00009B/864